How two months affected two years of bad
decisions, regrets, health issues, constant stress,
mass money gains, mass money loss and how I
healed through it all.

MY LOXI
GIRL

D1518177

Two Year Memc

MARIE STRIDE

This book contains content that might be troubling to some readers including, but not limited to, depictions of mental health, sickness, neglect, and depression/anxiety. Please be mindful of these and other possible triggers and seek assistance, if needed, from a medical health professional.

To My Loxi Girl who healed me.

To My YouTube Subscribers who brought sunshine
to my stormy days.

PART I

I lead a small life. I don't think it's overly complicated or overly exciting perhaps compared to others; yes it's just small but it's mine. My life isn't perfect and I make mistakes and I go through struggles but one thing I that is a usual constant in my life is that I tend to always make the best decisions for myself.

Until recently.

I made one bad call and since then it's been a case of the domino effect.

These chapters will reflect the past two years of my life. From losing my dog which triggered my first time experiencing panic and anxiety to my stomach health spiraling and moving out of my home state of Texas to Florida. Trying to heal from the loss of Loxi and then ending up struggling with my decisions, regrets, mass money gains and mass money loss, and how it all lead me back to home.

I'm self publishing this book, so don't judge me too hard for any editing/grammar issues that might come up during your reading.

I hope you are cozy and I hope you enjoy this book.

Over the course of my life I have heard many statements like this:

"I have been called to do…"

This has always mystified me. I envy the people who know without a doubt that they felt some type of calling to do something…anything, because I have felt like, in my life, I am just going through blindly trying to figure it all out on my own.

How did you know you were called to do something by God? How did you know that?

How did you know he asked you to do something?

That always puzzled me so much because even though I am spiritual and was raised Roman Catholic, I always struggled with hearing God, or knowing when I am meant to do something.

Instead, I have felt as if I have been mostly alone in my life even. Yes I know God is beside me but I never hear Him, sometimes I never feel Him, and through some of my darkest moments these past two years I have even felt abandoned by Him.

Only recently have I realized that this may be the lesson He had planned for me all along.

As if my journey was all about isolating me from people, relationships and even Himself because this is where He wants me to grow. This is where I *needed* to grow.

In my faith.

June of 2021 is when the spiraling began. When my Loxi girl passed away.

My girl, my dog, my soul mate.

But it would be August when all the stress and trauma of her loss would catch up to my mind and body.

In those two months everything would change in my life. I would go down the darkest road I had ever traveled.

After Loxi died leading up to August, without knowing, my body would begin to break down because the stress I was going through made my entire body fall apart. I started to experience things I had never experienced before like panic attacks and my stomach (which historically had always been a mess in my early childhood days) had only gotten worse. I didn't even know my stomach pains could honestly get any worse but life proved me wrong.

What no one knew who watched me on YouTube was that I was constantly going to the ER which I never disclosed on camera because I kept it all hidden away.

If you just found my book on Amazon and know nothing about me, my name is Marie and I have two YouTube channels: CraftyGirl and CraftyGirl Vlogs.

When I turned that camera on no one would know what was really happening behind the scenes. How hard I struggled mentally and physically.

Nothing I had ever gone through with my stomach could compare to what began to happen to me after Loxi's death.

Sometimes now I forget how painful it was, almost as if my brain is in self protection mode and doesn't want me to travel back to those times because it was unbearable.

The amount of times my daughter had to see me in the state I was in is what honestly saddens me the most. Forget my pain, forget what I was going through, but for my daughter to see me in that condition? The worst.

For HER to be the adult, for HER to be strong and watch her mother who is a type A perfectionist who always has it together fall apart like that…I can't even imagine what her thoughts were.

She was used to me being strong, independent, and hard working. That was all she saw and the mother she knew. Her friends would often joke "Mikah's mom is in her office" because that is where I always was. Mikah had never seen me fall apart like this before.

My daughter wasn't used to seeing my eyes glaze over as I let myself fall into depression, watch me unable to get out of bed, watch me protect my dogs teddy bear's from being touched so her scent would remain on them and then cry my eyes out if they ever moved an inch.

I would scream and say that they had to remain exactly where they were because that was where Loxi last put them.

I was in heavy denial about her death. But that wasn't all my daughter experienced. She lost Loxi too but she also lost me.

She would hear her phone text alert go off coming from downstairs, coming from me telling her I was sick and I needed to go to the hospital at all hours of the night.

She would come down faithfully, like the good daughter she is and she would get me into her car, my body shaking, feeling like I'm going to black out from the pain which felt like an intense version of food poisoning while my body shook, while I cried in the car on the way to the hospital…no child should ever have to see that.

She did.

Several times I made it into the ER and I would get diagnosed with acute gastritis which is a sudden inflammation or swelling in the lining of the stomach. Other times, I never made it into the ER.

And on top of the stomach issues getting worse a new issue occurred in my body. In my mind.

Panic attacks.

And I have never experienced panic or anxiety in my life before. I was always the person who had it together. I was a perfectionist and multi-tasker through and through. I didn't have time to panic. I was a single mom and I mean *single* mom with no dad raising her at a time where family was scattered throughout the US so I didn't have the village I needed during those early years.

So when I got sick? Didn't matter, I still had to get up, take care of her, take her to school and keep going, keep going to work because if I didn't bills wouldn't be paid. And then where would we be?

A time where the corporate jobs I had didn't care that I was a single mom. Companies got away with much more back in those days than now but if I wasn't in my seat by 8am it was an automatic write up, these companies never cared about me or my personal life. As long as I showed up and made money for the big guy that was all I was good for, while teachers and daycare sitters got to have my daughter more than I did. I struggled with this a lot.

I was always punctual, always had to-do lists, and I was always only thinking of that day. I couldn't even think of the future because I was too busy.

So when the panic started...for a controlled person like myself? It only made it ten times worse because that control I needed was no longer in my grasp.

And that made me snap.

And what's interesting about panic attacks that I discovered is that regardless of how significant or minor the events occur in your life that trigger anxiety, panic is panic. Is losing a dog the same as losing a human? Most times the answer is no; one is an animal the other obviously a human being but there are times when if that pet is your life it can be pain just as great. Regardless, losing my dog triggered panic attacks and even on my better days it sneaks up on you for no reason, no triggers and it just happens regardless if you want it to or not.

I knew that I had some sort of imbalance in my brain most likely caused by the stress I was holding in my body that was causing this new feeling. Just because I woke up and had a better day and I laughed and smiled didn't mean that in seconds I wasn't feeling like my world was ending because my brain is firing signals I can't seem to control.

I noticed it when I would go for a neighborhood walk or bike ride and suddenly panic hits and I have to get home immediately. And that's not me. Most who know me or watch me know I love being outside. Running, biking, walking…

Those are my things and suddenly I can't do them anymore.

I felt as if I had no idea who I was. I felt a stranger to even myself because this version of me I no longer recognized. It was one of the scariest feelings in the world to me.

I remember being only a few streets away from home and feeling like I had to race home, like children playing tag and there was some home base where you were safe from being tagged out. I had to race back to my home base as if getting there meant the panic would stop.

And combined with my stomach problems, I felt as if my control had simply vanished. If I couldn't even control my own damn feelings, then what was I doing? Life didn't make sense to me. Was this what I had to expect out of my life? Stomach pains, panic attacks, and maybe if my body was kind to me I might have a few good hours? No, I couldn't handle that. I wanted full control over myself. I should have a human right to myself. So when I lost it and I no longer recognized the girl in the mirror it only made me fall that much harder.

Yes I knew even at the time things could have been worse, so yes I was lucky and grateful to just be breathing. To have all of my limbs, and to be able to walk and talk, see and smell, but I learned that even though society sometimes tries to make you feel as if you can't hurt because you are better off than most, I learned that you can simultaneously be grateful while going through pain. While being confused and upset and wanting to be mad at the world.

Sure sitting here now, now that I don't have those pains, now that all of this is in the past, it's so easy to say "well I definitely could have handled this better" or "I really didn't need to be that dramatic" but in that moment with my stomach hurting so much it was impossible to do much of anything, to have your mind trigger panic attacks with or without your consent, to feel the loss of someone who loved you so purely and unconditionally, you really feel pushed past beyond your limits.

I felt as if I no longer owned myself, I no longer had control over myself and something or someone else ruled me and I felt as if I had died mentally and in my place was someone I no longer recognized. Because now this panic was controlling me and I was a slave to it and the person I had always been, the strong independent me was now a shell of a lost soul.

I felt as if I was in a black space with nothing and no one around me because Loxi was gone, because my body and mind were falling apart on me, but I knew, the fighter in me, that I had to find my way out. By myself. Per usual.

I resented that at the time.

I had always done everything by myself. I raised myself, I took care of my daughter myself, I had only my income to rely on. Pay the bills, take care of the car, figure out what's wrong with the toilet or the disposal, get the grocery shopping done, clean the house, make breakfast lunch and dinner...I was just so damn tired of doing it all by myself.

Shouldn't someone owe me help?

Shouldn't someone take care of me for once in my life?

Those were the things I selfishly thought of even though deep down I knew that it was *my* decision of being alone that kept *me* alone. And yet I expected who and what to help me?

I thought those things because I pitied myself, because I wanted to fester in horrible feelings. Feeling horrible felt right because I lost my Loxi girl so any other issues I had I was simply negative about it. Because feeling good felt wrong. And feeling wrong felt better.

When you hit these dark places a pity party goes into full swing. But I'm not embarrassed by this. I think how I felt, even feeling sorry for myself in that moment is only natural. I was doing my best to just be human.

One of the best things I have learned in these past two years is to simply stop being so hard on myself. You always hear that you have to love yourself before you can love anyone else. Sounds pretty logical right? Open shut case makes total sense but the more I thought about that the more I realized maybe I don't know what it actually means to love myself? I would recognize that I "loved" myself but why wasn't it working?

I think the journey of figuring out how to love yourself is going to vary person to person and I learned that one of the ways I needed to love myself was to stop being so hard on me. It wasn't just "oh hey, feel good about yourself, LOVE yourself" word affirmations, no it was more than that to get there for me.

It was taking certain actions for myself or against myself and I had to stop being so hard and critical of every move I made.

But when the panic hits, there is no loving me. I am hating myself more and more every day and every day I submerge myself further into every negative thought I can have.

And all the while, I'm filming videos. You could go back during August of 2021 and go through until about December of 2021 and in that time frame I'm at the worst I have ever been in my life yet I don't think anyone would be able to tell how bad I was.

This goes to show that social media isn't what it's all cracked out to be. It wasn't that I didn't want to share these things, it was that my channel was a happy place, a safe place for you to visit and feel good. Not to watch me lose it.

I couldn't put out what I was going through when I thought about how many messages and how emails I got on the daily of people telling me how my videos help them throughout their day and how rough some of your lives were going. How much impact I have had and I just couldn't stomach going on camera and bringing my negativity to them. I couldn't do it.

Looking back now, deciding not to share it for that reason was what had actually kept me sane.

I felt as if I was protecting you guys from my problems and not putting it in on your hearts while also giving me a reason to escape my issues.

You were my safe place.

For those that remember my words, how often have I said you guys don't know what you mean to me. How you saved me. This is what I mean. This is the book that will explain that.

You kept me from that final break I knew if it had occurred, I could never recover from. And I will forever be grateful to you. You were my last straw that remained strong.

When I watch myself back during that time, I don't see life in my eyes but it kept me going. It kept a part of my mind occupied just enough that I didn't just lose what control over myself I did have left.

Let's start from the beginning again...so the darkness in my life began when I lost Loxi.

Loxeigh Blue aka Loxi.

The life in my eyes left me when Loxi took her last breath which I used to replay over and over and over for months. I can hear it even now when I close my eyes. I can see the gentle look in her eyes that she kept pinned on me in those last hours of her life.

I made myself replay that moment as a form of punishment.

I was her voice and I failed her and that was all I saw. I never liked her Vet and most of my long time subscribers might remember the time Loxi had stomach issues and my vet clearly was not doing anything about it. I look back at that and I know that is when the cancer really started to take form and it just fell through the cracks. I should have pushed harder for an x-ray or blood work and I didn't.

And because of this I punished myself because my dog can't speak for herself. She can't tell anyone she doesn't feel good or that something is off. It was my job to make sure she was healthy and happy.

And because I didn't do that, I had been told by that same vet (I couldn't stand) the day I found out that he could put her down right then and there. DISGUSTED. That was what he advised.

That her quality of life was over.

I almost passed out physically- this was during COVID-19 so I couldn't go into the vet's office with her. I had dropped her off and went to the grocery store and then got the call. By the time I pulled up to the vets office I was hyperventilating. I had never hyperventilated before and I truly started to see stars, black spots and both of my hands almost up to my elbows went completely numb. I remember thinking to myself to breath because if I passed out in my car no one would be able to help me because my doors were locked. I my body was shutting down and my brain was quickly trying to resolve the issue, I remember this clear as day. Because my mind was working but my body was completely shutting down so I remember thinking I couldn't reach over to unlock my doors, so I forced myself to begin breathing. So I began to breath and when I could speak again I told him to bring my dog to me.

That is what I said to that monster. "Don't touch her. Bring me my dog"

Loxi gave me two months from that day. Two beautiful months and made it to her 9th birthday. When it should have been days, maybe two weeks. She gave me two months.

She stayed as long as she could for me until the day I looked at her and I knew she had had enough.

I sometimes think I don't know what's worse, a tragic death or one you know that's coming. I have experienced both from a pet perspective. My previous dog, Lolly, died tragically. One morning she was with me having a normal day and the next day she was gone.

With Loxi I had to watch her slip away from me. Sometimes I think the death you know is coming might be worse. That day I looked at her after sleeping with her on the couch all night, her breathing very labored because the cancer was all over her lungs and organs, I woke up and she looked at me like she was telling me it was ok.

And I couldn't let her hurt anymore. Not for me. It was time to stop being selfish, it was time to send her home.

But was she truly ready? Did she have a few more days or weeks in her? I simply couldn't tell. I had gone to Lubbock and taken Loxi with me and that was when her erratic breathing had begun so I took her to a vet there. He was absolutely wonderful and loved Loxi.

For those that loved Loxi furiously I want you to know how wonderful this man was. He treated our girl RIGHT.

He gave her a steroid shot, what my original vet should have done and didn't even do for her!

And boy did it change Loxi. Only for a few days because the cancer burned through the steroid, but in those few days Loxi was herself again. She was running around doing her usual shenanigans.

I felt hope, I thought maybe Loxi will live.

I had completely changed her diet. Sugar feeds cancer so I immediately cut out her kibble food which has sugar in it. Loxi's diet now consisted of filtered spring water, cooked chicken and rice. That was it.

But it was too late. Her cancer was already aggressive and all over her body. I saw this from the vet in Lubbock who showed me her x-ray, when my previous vet couldn't even do that for me.

This vet in Lubbock told me that I would know it was time if Loxi lost the following three qualities of life: Drinking, pooping, and walking. If she stopped doing those three things, that was when I would know it was time. Also something the original vet never shared with me. He just said "I'll put her down for you today"

Excuse me? Do you even like your job?

First thing I noticed was the pooping. It wasn't right. Then it was the walking...and boy did Loxi try. She wanted to follow me everywhere and she really did give me everything she had left in her tank. Absolutely everything.

Aren't pets the most beautiful thing on this planet? I just never understood why *their* lives have to be so short.

I believe it was a Friday morning when I knew, knew that she had given me everything she could and she had nothing left, yet she would have kept going and going and going.

So the pain I felt making that decision and then loading her up into my car knowing she wasn't going to come back home did permanent damage to me. I won't fully heal from this wound until I see her again.

And when she got out of my car for the last time and I know my brain is ticking and logging all of these "last" moments, my own personal death was already beginning. She stayed by my side the entire time, resting her head on my foot as I sat down on the floor with her. Mikah stayed in the room with us until it was time. Mikah couldn't bare it, she had to leave the room.

I held her, my face buried into her body, her heart still beating and all I can do in this moment is repeat the same thing over and over and over.

"I love you."

The memories of our time together didn't seem like I had enough stored. I needed more, I needed more time. Nine years wasn't enough.

Loxi was my little sidekick, like most of our pets are to us.. She was with me through it all.

The good days, the bad days, the rainy days, the holidays, the knife nights (wink wink). She laid at my feet when I worked countless hours in my office. She waited for me when I had to leave home to go work in the office at the time I had a corporate job. She greeted me so happily when I came from a business trip, she curled up with me on the couch and watched movies with me. She identified ghosts in my house, and was up to no good when I filmed in that kitchen of that one house…those who know, know.

But my favorite memory of all? When we had no power during the Texas ice storm. I hated winter but that year…that last winter I didn't know I was going to have with her ironically enough made me fall in love with winter. And it was because of Loxi. I don't know what it was, maybe my angel guides steering me and Loxi into this experience together because they knew it would be our last but boy did I love every minute of that awfully miserable no heat frozen house ice storm. Because I had her. Because my Loxi girl was by my side. I felt like with Loxi, I could do anything.

The joy I had, wrapping that plaid scarf I made her and putting my matching one around myself and walking us carefully outside on the ice. I love that winter because I loved being with her.

For Loxi's earlier years Mikah was in middle school and then high school so a lot of my attention obviously was on my child. I grew closer with Loxi when Mikah left for college and I felt as if our bond had deepened but it was ripped from me way too soon.

I didn't know a few short months later I would hold her and tell her I loved her for the very last time.

I said it over and over because it was the only important thing I wanted her to know. And those were my last words to her.

Even though they are put into a restful sleep, you are losing them before that. Because once they are asleep that's it, they aren't waking up from that. So the goodbyes happened before. But saying I love then when she was awake to hear me still wasn't enough.

I need to get as many I love you's as I can so she can hear me. So she can know she's not alone, that I was with her to the very end. To that last breath. So she knows that I love her. It's the only important thing I can say to her.

Did you know that her original name was Venus?

The goddess of love and beauty.

It's fitting, don't you think?

I drove twice to Houston to get her. The first time I showed up and picked up each puppy in the litter even though prior to my drive I had already picked her out. However, when I got there, I couldn't tell which one she was, so many of them looked exactly the same. Loxi was last and when I picked her up she kissed me. The other dogs didn't. I knew she was the one, I even thought to myself "even if this isn't Venus, this is the one I want" and when I was told it was Venus I just knew she was MY baby. So I was devastated when I found out she was too young and the owner had gotten her two litters confused. One was six weeks old and the other litter was too young for pick up. And I was adamant that I wanted HER. So I left without her and I was gutted.

I could have just chosen another dog from the six week liter, they were all equally adorable and beautiful but I wanted Loxi.

I waited several more weeks for her turn, six weeks before I could go back and get her and when I finally had her, she was worth the anxiety of waiting for her. I had just lost my Lolly and when Loxi licked me, I can't explain it but it was as if we had met in another lifetime.

She was always meant to be mine.

So letting her go broke me. What's crazy is that in that moment as I'm holding onto the most beautiful soul to ever grace this planet, another person is next to me and it's their job to do this and I don't even remember her.

I wish I could and I'm sorry I don't. But I remembered this: She was quiet and let me have my time with my girl. Let me have those final last moments without drawing attention to herself while I cradled Loxi in my arms, letting me have those final moments in her peaceful sleep so I wouldn't have to let go just yet as I listened to her even soft breaths so different from the panting only moments before. Now I can't help but wonder how much this hurt this woman to watch this. To watch a part of me die with my dog.

I remember telling this woman "Not yet"

To carry this as a burden from having a job like that? It takes a special person to do this. To see heartbreak on a daily basis. I am forever grateful for those that take on jobs like this. I'm sorry you carry all of this weight with you. I hope you find a way to release it and not carry this with you.

After she left me alone with Loxi, though she was already entering the rainbow bridge, Mikah came back to hold Loxi one last time.

I blamed myself for her death. And the more I punished myself the worse I got. My body could only take so much.

In this time of my life…I realized just how dependent I was on Loxi.

I stopped dating around 2012. Yes, I stopped dating for over ten years. But it was a choice I had made. It was one of my most asked questions when I would do my rare Q&A's at the time was how do I handle being alone for so long?

To me I didn't see a problem. I was happy being alone. I LOVED being alone. No one could hurt me that way so to me it made logical sense. And pets, pets never hurt us, even if we hurt them. They are so loving and innocent and want to make us happy. Loxi never hurt me.

And I kept my girl high on her pedestal, where she deserved to be.

My last relationship obviously failed, and at the time my daughter Mikah was going into the 8th grade or 9th. And I remember thinking, I'm tired of dating. It just sucked up so much time, it's mentally taxing and I just wanted to watch the only child I knew I would have gone through high school. I had heard all about how time flies so I decided I wouldn't date for four years so I could focus on her instead. Once she got through high school, I realized I was having way too much fun being alone to want to go back out into the dating world.

I liked not having couple fights. I liked not having insecure feelings. I liked not second guessing what I was wearing and if I was pretty enough. I liked having control of the remote, I liked having my own space. Hell, I liked eating ugly in peace. Not wearing makeup, and just not feeling that constant feeling of relationship anxiety and disappointments. It was so damn nice for a change to just feel happy and not get my feelings hurt.

So then my daughter continues onto college.

So in my life I had Mikah (but she was off at Texas Tech) I had you guys, I had my brother, my mom, and I had Loxi.

That was it.

That was my life. And it seemed like enough. It was...until Loxi was removed from the equation.

And then the math stopped adding up.

And when Loxi passed and my world went dark, I knew then just how much I actually depended on her. How much was truly broken in my world.

You see, with my daughter off at college and living alone, while yes Loxi was a dog, she was still a breathing living soul and while she couldn't talk back to me, she was still providing me comfort and love. She was my best friend. I would find myself rushing home from running errands just to be with her. It sounds bizarre but when I think of the movie Cast Away and Tom Hanks befriends a volleyball I completely understand that now.

It's not silly. When you're in survival mode as a human being, you have to have some form of interaction that mimics what you would get from another human being. If you don't have that option to have an interaction with another living breathing person, then you find it in something else. A pet, an object, a place...

Regardless of what you connect to, the human needs something or someone. Even if it's not another human being. Loxi was that part of the equation for me. The part that filled a void.

So losing her turned my world upside down because she was crucial to what kept me together.

I remember coming home that day after saying goodbye and it had stormed. Not just rain...but a full on massive storm.

So this was in a way Day 1 of when my body would take a turn. This is just one of many things that I would do that causes a tremendous amount of stress on my body. This somehow perfectly timed storm triggered my panic.

As thunder and lightning struck what seemed like all around me and only me, and all I could do was scream and cry that Loxi was at that vet's office all alone. You see, she hated storms.

So on that way back without her, I went into a place where I looked at Mikah and I said "We didn't have a choice…right? She couldn't keep going on. I couldn't let her be in pain anymore."

Mikah somberly nodded in agreement but that ride back I was in denial and I was numb and I was convincing myself that it was the right decision.

But the moment I walked into that house and saw her bed…I lost it. I curled up into her spot and cried.

And then a few hours later the storm began.

And I lost it even more. There is no way around this to describe it to you. I lost my damn mind.

I was up pacing and crying and shaking. Loxi was alone.

It frightened her so much that whenever it stormed she was always allowed on my bed so I could comfort her.

And even though she was gone and happily playing beyond the rainbow bridge, I was on earth trying to grab my car keys so I could what? Break into a vet's office at night to hold her? I felt as if I had left her there to be scared because my mind still couldn't place the fact that she was gone. That she no longer had cancer eating away at her, that she was in the highest of kingdoms in a place where she always deserved to be.

No, my mind still had not recognized that she had gone peacefully. Instead my mind said she was at this vets office all alone, cold and scared because I couldn't fight her cancer for her like I should have. She was there because of me. That's not a pity party. That's the truth. One I have had to accept.

I question this: Why did it have to storm that night?

I look back on that now and wonder if that storm was brought just to me from God to lead me to where I am today. Maybe that's silly, but maybe it's not.

That storm lead me to spiral. It was what kicked it all into motion. What made the panic start, what made me sick, all the hospital trips, all the times I sat and stared and did nothing. And the spiraling forced me to look at my life and begin to fix things.

That night I cried myself to sleep. I kept telling Loxi I was so sorry. Sorry that I had left her there all alone and told her not to be scared. I needed to believe she was still alive. I couldn't entertain reality that night.

My mind clearly was in protection mode or most likely denial mode. Both.

And what's crazy is that I FELT Loxi that night. I can't explain it, it's the craziest experience I ever had, but I swear she was there on my bed.

It wasn't just a feeling, I am 100% sure I heard her get onto my bed as I cried. I remember looking up because I heard her body rustling against the side of the bed before she jumped.

And now I realize my little baby finally went home to her rainbow but all to come back to ME and COMFORT ME a few short hours later.

Loxi did that. She did everything for me. She even held on just for me. She had been ready to go long before I could let her go. On her last walk, she still followed me faithfully. Slowly, painfully, but faithfully. Loxi quite literally would follow me anywhere. And she did. And you know what? I would follow HER anywhere. Ever see the movie What Dreams May Come with Robin Williams? I would have gone to the depths of hell to get her.

I never deserved her. But I'm humbled that God thought so.

The effects of all of this stress took two months from the day she died. Two months of day in and day out of crying, pain, torment, flashes of her very last breath before my body started to break down and tell me it couldn't take anymore. My body was in fight or flight and it was definitely fighting for it's life.

It wasn't until one night that I will never forget when it all began to change.

Another late night trip to the ER. I had been to the hospital multiple times since Loxi passed away. This night I wake up and I'm in pain. Unbearable stomach pains and I call out for Mikah. It's barely eight pm but I learned a hack. That if I went to sleep early, I didn't have to FEEL anything. I didn't have to THINK anything. Sleep was my best friend. I wanted it all the time. It was like doing drugs maybe, because I escaped reality, didn't want to deal, so I did my drug to patch it up. I slept. Instead of addressing the issue like I should have. Well that night, I would finally crack and be forced to address the issue.

It's so bad I can't walk. I don't know how I get on sweats and a sweater and socks so I can be warm in the hospital but that's what I'm thinking. I need to be warm.

She helps me walk out to her car like I'm a frail. Because I am. At this point I have made several trips to the ER. Many actually.

And sometimes I never go in. Mikah drives me there and I cry myself out of going in. I'm afraid they will think I'm weak, I'm afraid they will think I'm crazy so I cry as I stare at the Emergency doors wanting to go in so bad but I can't get myself to waste those Nurses time. Waste the doctors time when they have *real* emergencies.

Is mine real?

And that's what happens this last and final time. She gets me into her passenger seat, it's probably somewhere around 8pm, I don't actually remember the time. But I cry all over again. Because it's the same struggle. Am I so bad that I need to go in there? Or am I going to stare at the doors and cry and wish I could go in there and let them take my stomach pains away?

I am covered head to toe because remember I have had stomach issues my entire life. This process isn't new to me. Most of you might remember the year I had my appendix almost rupture. Good times.

I have had a bad stomach my entire life, so one thing for me is to be warm. Warmth helps like a heating pad. So even though the stomach pains are making me want to black out, I put on my sweatpants, I put on my sweater and I remember how slowly I moved. I could barely walk.

So she drives me like the good daughter that she is trying to make me feel better but knows there is nothing she can do but stare at me, and we get to the ER and I stare longingly at those doors.

I want in so bad.

I can't do it. I don't want to be judged, I don't want to be looked at as weak.

My entire life I have been in ER's more times than I care to admit. If I had to guess a number I would say well over 30 times in the course of my life including this period of my life.

So I tell her I'm not going in, I can't do it and she drives us back home and that is when I snap. I'm curled up against the door my face pressed to the glass as I cry quietly looking up at all the lights. Christmas lights. I have never felt less like my self. Like the real me died with Loxi. And in my original place is some person I no longer recognize. I'm frail, I'm fragile, I'm empty, and I no longer have control over my mind.

And as we enter our neighborhood I can see into people's homes.

And I cry like I have never ever in my life cried before. It was more than a sob, it was more than tears, it was gut wrenching because inside those homes I think no one is experiencing what I am in that moment.

And I never hated my life more. I have never really been an envious person. I liked my little life, I thought it was cute and cozy and I was so grateful for it. But that night, I was so damn tired of being sick.

I remember screaming, crying, racked with sobs so hard that I can't breath, that I want to be those people SO BAD. I have never cried so loud in my life and I think I remember touching the window in pain as I cried "I want to be them. Why can't I be them?" I don't think I ever felt so low in my life.

I wish I could describe it but it was as simple as I was just so sad. I remember putting my head against the window and just feeling so sorry for myself.

I know people have it worse, people losing their loved ones and having cancer and I mean this in no disrespect but it didn't mean that what I was going through also wasn't hard. That was another thing I struggled with the past two years. This thought in my head like "you shouldn't feel this, because others have it worse" but I learned that I had to separate that from myself. I couldn't control what others were going through, I only had my two feet to walk in front of the other and I had to stop feeling guilty for struggling with my own personal life journey.

So here I am in that moment that broke me.. It was the last and final straw. I had nothing left. I was breathing but my heart wasn't beating.

My body was in pain, I couldn't leave the house, and my daughter watched her mom metaphorically drown, I had fallen about as far as I could mentally go.

It might not seem significant but in that moment, I became angry. I was so angry for everyone in their homes not being sick like me. I was angry with God that I had spent 40 years on this earth and it was always some damn stomach pain. HOW MUCH MORE could I take?

The answer was zero. I couldn't take it anymore. Looking into those homes, I snapped.

I couldn't understand why I was going through this.

I simply could no longer accept that this was my life.

I had a lot to be grateful for. I always felt grateful for each day of my life. There usually isn't a day that goes by, even now, that I wake up and I'm like "wow, God has gifted me another day" And yes stomach problems, anxiety issues, but overall health is "good". I was lucky to not be in a hospital like others fighting for their life, or others waking up that day and finding out a devastating diagnosis or losing a loved one, or losing a source of income/job. Yes I knew deep down how lucky I was and that someone in life always has it worse, but that didn't mean what I was going through didn't hurt both physically and mentally.

And when I hit this place where my mind hurt, my stomach hurt so much I didn't feel like I was living as well as I could I knew I was hanging on by a thread. I could handle my stomach issues for the most part but when I coupled that with my mind feeling weak and not even being able to control that...it was an experience I didn't know how to handle.

It kept storming and storming in my life and I needed the sun because I knew if I kept this up, I was going to go in a very dangerous path in my mind and I had to get a grip.

PART II

Maybe my experience of losing a dog seems so small and insignificant. Someone reading this for sure without a doubt has had it way harder than I have. But regardless of what caused the pain, it was still very real and it felt unbearable and it started to affect me more than just mentally. It was now having a physical impact on my body.

Loxi was everything to me.

She was my entire world and that world exploded after our final goodbyes. This isn't just about Loxi, this is also about me finding out that maybe I was lonelier than I thought and her death shattered my little safe bubble I put myself in. About discovering what my life was missing, what I am not capable of, what I am capable of and figuring out my life's purpose. Loxi happened to be a gift from God that was the violent push to make me see what I refused to see or really what I couldn't see.

I wouldn't be where I am today without experiencing her loss.

After that night in Mikah's car when I couldn't bring myself to go into the ER where I sobbed in a way I want to forget but never will, I knew something had to change. As I sobbed uncontrollably, never more jealous of strangers in my entire life, I knew I was done because I was having some weird out of body experience. I was sick, my stomach hurt, I was balling my eyes out and still my mind in that moment was thinking "You can't push yourself further than this. It's too much" because what the hell do strangers have to do with me and my life? They weren't responsible for me, my mind or my body.

I was responsible for that.

So I knew my reaction to strangers meant I had a bigger issue at hand. I wanted to just feel good. Don't we all though? I wanted for everything to feel great, for me to have everything I wanted and for life to simply hand it to me.

Wrong. So very wrong. I learned that even as I type this now I will face more life challenges but it's how I deal with them that matters.

I spent two months after my dogs passing crying so much that the stress internalized into severe stomach pains. They say your stomach is your second brain and my body was clearly telling me that all the crying, all the sadness and the way I held all of this in was actually affecting me physically. Stomach produces serotonin and the production of serotonin controls your mood and is responsible for happiness.

So clearly if I'm under an immense amount of stress my serotonin isn't going to produce as much as it should. So there goes my mood and there goes my happiness.

I am not sure or concrete on how true these scientific statements are but I read somewhere that certain emotions are stored in certain organs.

Stress is stored in the brain/heart.
Worry in the stomach.
Anger in the liver.

And something is stored in the lungs but I couldn't remember what that one was.

All I knew was that I couldn't do this anymore. I had to fight my way back to myself.

It was all I wanted because the person I was in that moment was so fragile that if I kept going at that pace I wouldn't be able to work. And if I couldn't work how could I pay my bills? I don't have a husband to count on, or another source of income. All I had was myself so I knew it was time to care for me because that was my responsibility.

I had lost Loxi, if I lost myself then what quality of life did I have? God kept giving me a new day after new day and I wanted to fight for that. To be grateful for that but I also wanted to live it to my fullest. I didn't want to sit in this stress and constant pain.

I didn't want to be codependent on something or someone else because at the end of the day I am in charge of myself, my health, my happiness.

I wanted the OLD ME back because what I was becoming was something I didn't recognize at all and that scared me the most. I spent 40 years with myself and suddenly who I was was so beyond unrecognizable it made me scared enough to go to counseling. Which I later ended up doing.

I only visited this counselor a few times. It was a man and I liked him well enough but I just knew in the end it wasn't right for me. I wanted to take care of me because I simply lost faith in Doctors and I grouped this counselor in that category. He simply didn't understand me and he was great but like I said didn't work for me. We started with panic attacks. He gave sound advice and I listened and I tried it but it didn't work for me. He advised that when I felt the panic coming on that I needed to trigger some other type of sensory. Whether it was washing my hands (so feeling water touch my skin) or singing (vibration in my throat) things like that and trust me I tried them all. Didn't work for me. It might work for others because at the end of the day we are all wired differently. Just because something might work for me might not work for someone else and vice versa.

What I did get out of it that I liked was simply having someone to unload on.

But even then I had a lot to address. My stomach, my mind, the lack of control, the loss of Loxi. At the time I didn't even see it that way. I didn't see it as a checklist. And because I didn't see it like a checklist, I didn't have the effects of feeling overwhelmed and I'm grateful for this. I simply knew I had to fix myself one day at a time and I had to start now.

I started with my panic attacks.

I went through countless hours of videos on YouTube and Tik Tok wanting to see other people like myself. Not a doctor, just a normal person giving us their own personal experience on tips and tricks and I found the art of dumping my face into a bowl of ice water.

So I start with doing this every single day.

While I do this I move onto my stomach. It was time to change how I ate.

And trust me, after forty years on this earth, I have cried many of times about this. You think I didn't know long before this that I had to change what I consumed? Oh I knew. But I hated it. I hated once again that other people could eat these things and be fine and I couldn't.

Why me?

It wasn't fair, so I refused to change how I ate. If other people could do it, then I deserved the same. That was my thought process. Stubborn.

And every little tiny thing I couldn't do, I blamed on God. I blamed strangers, I blamed everyone but *me*.

Why did I feel as if God had to separate me from his sheep? I wanted to be with the crowd, do what they did, eat what they ate but instead I felt as if I was always different and not in a good way. I was kept in constant isolation in every form without realizing it. Like no matter how many times I got close to a crowd I was yanked back and was reminded to be humbled.

"No, no...you don't belong in a place of feeling good...go back to the pain where you belong"

That is what I felt like.

And it hurt. It still hurts if I'm being honest. It hurts that I was always meant to be pulled back to my own space without anyone in it.

I really started to form a deeper relationship with God around 2016, started to have my own personal relationship with Him outside of Church. Outside of what pastors were saying.

Nothing wrong with that, I was born and raised Roman Catholic in a very Italian style. Rosarie, praying to the Virgin Mary, the works.

But I realized that for me, it wasn't my spiritual journey. It made me constantly feel as if I was never good enough for Him or Jesus. That I was a sinner, I would constantly sin, and I couldn't be the daughter He wanted me to be and showing up to church made me feel like an impostor. I know that is not the case. That church isn't bad, that it's a place for EVERYONE no matter the circumstances. I just simply learned it wasn't working for me. I felt as if I had some superficial relationship with God. Like ok, showed up to Church, listened to your word, I'm going to go sin again and I'll see you later. I'll pray when I need something.

My mind just kept telling me I wasn't good enough. Then one day I heard someone say "talk to Him as if He is your best friend. That's what He wants"

And that my friends changed the entire game for me.

And that is what I have been doing since. I keep my relationship with Him and Jesus in me. In my mind, in my heart, in my prayers and I talk very openly, very raw, very honest with Them.

And it feels so good.

I don't have to be perfect, I can yell and scream at Him when I'm angry, I can pray and request the same thing over and over till I'm blue in the face, and I can be selfish and sometimes only pray for me, and sometimes pray others, and I know I am still loved. It's the most free

I have ever felt and in turn it has made me want to do better as a human being. To be kinder, to be forgiving, to be giving. And I have grown closer to Him. It wasn't that I wanted to scream and yell at Him, it was that I didn't have to feel fake or perfect, I mean why not just be myself? He sees what is in my heart anyway so why hide what I know he already knew; and I never felt at peace like this in my entire life. God's peace.

But even in this change, I have noticed one thing. I still rarely feel His presence. I can count on one hand how often I have truly felt Him.
But now I know why.
He wanted to fully isolate me. To grow in my faith…because while I never felt Him, it didn't mean he wasn't actually there. He was not only always there, but He had never left my side. Always by my side, watching me, holding me, soothing me, during times I screamed for Him and didn't feel Him and during times I completely forgot to seek Him while I sat in my own selfishness.
He will never leave me nor forsake me. Never.
I still get jealous…sometimes I wonder how so many can feel Him so much, others say they can hear Him and I have never experienced that. It always amazes me like:
"how did you hear Him?"
"What did He sound like?"
"What exactly did He say?
Why do others get to feel him, hear him, and get clear cut precise direction from him while I sit in pain, misery, silence, confusion….?
I know now.
Because this is what He chose for *me*. I had to learn that no matter what others' relationships were with Him, this was MY relationship with Him and I had to have

unshakeable faith that He was still beside me regardless if I could hear, feel, or see.

The journey isn't about being isolated. It's about TRUSTING that He is always there no matter what life tries to tell me. I have to have full on blind faith that He is always with me.

It's December by the time I realize it's time to change. And my first step is to heal my body. Heal my panic attacks.

So I started deep diving and finding holistic approaches because in my personal journey I hated doctors. They never really helped me much and mostly misdiagnosed me and I never felt comfortable in their care. That was again just my own journey, I know they have helped so many others and by no means am I putting down good people who do want to help others heal but it was not my personal experience.

This happens when I go see this doctor, which I think I might even have talked about on a vlog, where I am so desperate to be rid of my anxiety that I want to be placed on medication. Because damn is anxiety and panic so damn scary. My brain thought "nope, get rid of this feeling and get rid of it now, no matter what it takes"

So I see this doctor and I don't even remember really what we talked about, it might be in a video but I remember him telling me something along the lines of how my anxiety is actually tied to my stomach and that I am not producing enough serotonin and other things my body should be producing and so because I lack those because my body is not producing enough it has triggered my anxiety. I do remember him telling me "I hate to break it to you but you have always had anxiety you just didn't know it until now because it's hereditary"

So I left with my prescription for Lexapro and when I stopped at the store to get it, I filled it and went home and then stared at the bottle.

And then I started to think about how he spoke about my body not producing what it needed to produce. And I stare at these pills full of chemicals and I think "Now how the hell does this make sense?"

How is this man made pill of chemicals going to produce something my body should be doing naturally on its own?

I am not suggesting anyone reevaluate their own medication because I am NOT. I am simply talking about my thought process and doing what was best for me.

And for me it didn't make sense. And I thought…well if my body is struggling to make serotonin , dopamine, oxytocin, and endorphins then it's time to do all the things that trigger those in my body. I need to help my body do it. Naturally.

And I'm going to do it without chemicals.

So I researched each of the four and what triggers those in the body and I started to do it.

One of the first things I remember doing was dipping my face into a bowl of ice cold water with ice cubes in it. It is known for basically helping to reset your mind and nervous system. It is known to reset your fight or flight response and sends blood rushing back to your brain, heart and lungs. This allows your heart rate to go down and your senses to return to normal. Blood flow allows for oxygen in the body and that is important.

Because all of the stress I had inside me put my body into a Fight or Flight response. And I knew I couldn't heal properly if my body was in that condition. I needed to get out of Fight or Flight and put my body in Rest and Digest in order to begin the healing process.

I dipped my face for 10-20 seconds four of five times and boy did I start to really see a huge difference.

I also discovered Ashwagandha. This is a supplement, a healthy natural supplement that helps your body deal with stress better and stress was the evil here. Stress causes physical damage and inflammation and I couldn't heal my body in an inflamed state.

I knew in order to fully heal I had to get my stress gone, I had to get out of Fight or Flight and lower inflammation drastically to begin to heal my mind and my stomach.

This was my new morning routine:

7:00am:

Get up and immediately head outside (no phones no scrolling - straight outside) I go out barefoot even if it's raining and I put my feet to the earth. If it's sunshine I walk barefoot to the center of my lawn, sit in a chair and let the sun soak into my face and eyes but only with early morning sun. This right here alone, I feel confident enough to say is what helped my body. It didn't need to have a guard up, that I was safe and it could let me go into Rest and Digest and begin to heal.

I also let the sun hit my bare stomach to produce serotonin.

7:30am:

After fresh air and grounding (feet on earth) I would go inside and take my morning supplements on an empty stomach. First one was probiotic and the second one L-glutamine. L-glutamine (and please know I am not a doctor and I could get some of these facts wrong) I think worked in a way that it repaired my gut lining. This I knew has been destroyed with me over 40 years of just having a horrible stomach. So I knew that my gut lining had to have the most attention and L-glutamine helped aid that repair. I would let those two supplements sit alone in my stomach so that I could get max absorption. I took these two with orange juice.

8:00am:

I took my next supplement while still on an empty stomach, Ashwagandha and I would stretch my body. I only had water and orange juice in the morning. I removed coffee all together from my diet at the time. I might have had it every now and then but I mostly brewed it just to smell it LOL.
Then I would dip my face into a bowl of ice cold water.

9am-12pm:

Go for walks outside. Just to get my body moving and mostly for my digestive system. Even though I didn't have anything in my stomach since the night before from around 4pm, maybe 6pm at the very latest. But my system was backed up and had years upon years of damage so I was having to go so easy. I put myself in a mindset that I had to treat my stomach as fragile as I could but I also had to remember I needed proper nutrients. I should have most definitely done this with proper Doctor care and instructions but I wanted to do this alone. It wasn't a perfect routine and it wasn't as healthy as it could have been but it worked for me.

12:00pm:

I would finally eat and at this time because my stomach was in such a bad place I was very limited to what I could eat without further irritating it. I wasn't healed fully, that would take time. Plus I wasn't hungry until then, so I was listening to my body tell me what it wanted.

I would have my yogurt bowl. Greek yogurt, granola, strawberry and banana and honey. That was all I could stomach. It kept me full all day

4:00pm:

I had chips a hoy cookies. Not healthy, full of chemicals but it was what I could handle at that time because I was still full from my yogurt. This was just the beginning stages.

Other than having the cookies, I wouldn't eat past 4pm. I did this because my bedtime was 8pm. This was when my body was just naturally tired because I was mentally exhausted. So if my bedtime was 8pm I made sure to not eat four hours prior to allow my body that time to digest…so that when I was asleep, my body had already spent energy in the digestive process and therefore my body could then focus on spending the energy it had to repair other issues. People don't realize how much energy your body actually uses to digest. And my stomach problems always occurred at night because I had too much to process.

So I had to stop eating long before bedtime.

This also drastically cut my healing time in half.

7:00pm:

Night time digestive walk. Walking to get my digestive system going and then heading back to the house and getting into my night time routine. Brushing my teeth, washing my face, and taking what I think is probably one of the biggest supplements to change me and that is Magnesium paired with Vitamin D.

This alone I know regulated my bowel movements, helped me sleep, and somehow pieced me back together. This combination is gold to me and I do all of these steps even to this day.

8:00pm:

Sleep.

I stayed on this food diet for a while. I no longer ate out, and my fridge looked very different during these times.

Slowly but surely my body started to get better.

I was also keeping track of my "bathroom" visits when it came to stomach pain and diarrhea. I started this monthly tracker (which I still keep on these pages because when I look back at this, I am still so surprised) I believe January of 2022. And as each day went by and as I kept up with my healing routine, as the stress began to leave my body, as my body began to get out of Fight or Flight and into Rest and Digest…guess what never happened to me again? Diarrhea.

I didn't have stomach pains again.

I cried and cried and cried when I realized I had gone ONE MONTH. When I went into February and realized I had no stomach issues in January, I simply could not believe it. I had never EVER experienced that. I even ber being seven years old and being on the toilet

, urty years… it took forty years to go one month. And
then one month turned into two, three, four, five… and
it's not been almost two years and no more stomach
pains.

Thank you God for giving me Loxi. Thank you for
bringing her home to you, thank You for pushing me to
finally heal myself. I give all the Glory to You.

Since then I have changed my diet and sometimes I
will have a burger, or chipotle, or ice cream which is
usually a no no, but I have it in moderation and I cut my
portions down a lot.

But I still primarily stick to my same yogurt bowl, I
have a lot of fruit for snacks, not really big on
vegetables, and to be honest I rarely eat dinner but it
works for me and works for my stomach. There is still a
lot of work here to do but I'm thriving and I finally got my
mind and body synced together.

PART III

So now that I am healing my mind and my stomach,
to scale back a few months to October of 2021…I find
Loki. Most of you know who he is and for those of you
that don't, he was my new puppy.

My angel boy.

The same breed as Loxi and crazy how he stumbled into my world. I will never forget the long drive I made to Maypearl, Texas to get him. And when I picked him up and held him, I knew he was mine.

His mom was a brown and black coat and his father was black with brown brindle (Loki is like his dad), neither of his parents had any white markings nor his siblings. Loki was the only one with a tiny white mark on his chest by his heart. Loxi had a white chest so Mikah and I like to think that it was Loxi's kiss, the mark she left on Loki to let me know it's ok. That she's ok and that she picked Loki just for me.

I had gotten him a little bed for the car ride and a blanket and a little toy because he was six weeks old but the entire two hour car ride home, he wanted only to be in my lap. He cried in his bed and tried to come to me so I picked him up and kept him in my lap and that is where he fell asleep peacefully.

Since then, Loki has been like velcro to me. He loves me more than I deserve but that is what pet's do right? They love us with such innocence and with a pure heart. I remember the first few months he slept on my actual face. He was either curled in my neck or slept his entire body on my face LOL.

He would do that now if he could but if he did I would die of suffocation because he's 130 lbs of muscle.

He brought light into my life back into my eyes.

Yes, I realized that I depended so much on Loxi for all those human interaction things we need as people and I knew I needed work in that area too but I was a dog girl. I would always be a dog girl even though I grew up with cats. Love cats, I love animals but even as a young girl with cats, I always knew I wanted a dog. So

Loki comes into my life and I have to name him. I want it to be close to Loxi. And I love Loki the villain from the Avengers so it just made sense.

I hit a moment with Loki and maybe this is morbid and maybe some of you have thought this or maybe some of you haven't...but after losing Loxi, I hit a moment where I looked at Loki and I thought "damn...I fell in love with him and it's going to hurt like hell to lose him"

I know it's not a thought you should sit on and keep thinking but I thought it when he crept up into my heart and took it over anyhow.I know it will hurt like hell, maybe even worse as it seems to get worse after each pet leaves us, but I know how lucky I am too. I'm lucky to have him now and I'll do anything to give him the best life I can. And that's all I can do.

I have had several thoughts where I thought "I'm too tired. I can't anymore"

This is why I'm writing this instead of doing a video. Because I knew I didn't have the guts to admit this. The part where I just didn't know what was left for me on this earth. It seemed as if my quality of life after Loxi's death seemed to diminish. I lost control, I felt sick all the time, it was hard getting up to know my day was going to be just like the last.

I felt alone, I felt unloved, I felt empty. Of the alone, unloved, and empty...the emptiness was the worst of the three. Loxi kept me company, Loxi loved me, Loxi filled my voids. I missed her.

In our last family vacation in Destin, I say this to a family member:

"Do you ever think that there is nothing that could possibly make you happy? But you think of everything possible that could and none of it sounds appealing?" Like winning the lottery, or finding the perfect spouse, etc…that even the thought of those things wouldn't bring you joy? And in which they responded with "I know exactly what you mean"

I have no idea why I said that to them but that's where my mind was. It was spiraling and I was hurting and I recognized that I sunk into a depression. I wanted to know if anyone else thought it too, and this person just happened to be next to me when I thought it, And something about them fully understanding me and how quickly they went into how that applied to them made me feel like maybe I wasn't alone.It made me feel better in the sense that I wasn't by myself even though I obviously didn't actually want someone to feel that way.

But that is where I was. I felt as if nothing in that moment in my life could make me happy. Sounds clearly of depression. Little things usually makes me the happiest. A movie, tv show, a certain YouTuber I like to watch, running, decorating…and at that time in my life, nothing made me happy. How does losing a dog create all of this chaos? Because maybe Loxi was covering the issues I kept buried away and without her there to keep me anchored, I eventually floated away.

This year I just felt so defeated. Yes the second half was swimming myself up to the surface because it was a struggle getting myself out of the negative mindset. And that was when I realized that my negative mind had just as much impact on me critically as the stress. It's the same form, but it's almost like self-inflicted stress. I realized that I had to stop talking to myself so horribly.

Which is hard to do when you also put yourself out publicly and you know you are being criticized and made fun of. Or called a liar or when strangers think they know every single thing that you do but they don't. It doesn't help when you're in a very weak place mentally but it was the women like you who were kind and patient and forgiving and cheered me on.

Who loved Loxi as hard as I did, who wanted to see me grow and thrive and be happy. You wanting that for me...kept me from going into that dark place in my mind where I knew it. I felt it, I even talked to my therapist about it, like there were times where I felt like if I allowed myself to go there, to have that one thought which was "I can't do this anymore, I'm going to lose my mind" I knew if I recognized that thought and let it be real, I wasn't going to recover. I spoke to that counselor about this and he told me "I can assure you that you won't lose your mind" because that was my biggest concern there.

Like that one thought was floating just on the edge of my mind and if I let it, I could easily go and open that door and let that thought in and it would take full control of me and that would be it.

I don't know why I went through this, I don't know why my mind which was always so "sound" just deserted me when I hit rock bottom. I was always together, I was always pushing myself for my goals and wanting to be successful so why is that I felt like my entire body just gave up on me during *one* hard time?

Maybe I wasn't as strong as I thought. Maybe I had pushed myself so hard that my body had always been right on the very cusp of falling apart if one bad thing happened. I clearly didn't take care of my mind properly because losing my dog turned my entire world upside down. I'm not saying that my love for her wasn't good enough to actually turn my world upside down, but I also think what happened to me went way too far.

During my therapy sessions at first, it was all about managing my panic attacks and the techniques he wanted me to try. Basically it was all about sensory. So if I felt panic coming in I was supposed to do something that would incorporate sensory. So either washing my hands (feeling the water on my skin) or singing (feeling the vibration in my throat) or walking outside and feeling the wind on my face etc... I have to admit I tried these techniques and I found they didn't really help me, however, when I started to dunk my face in a bowl of ice water that stopped my panic in the tracks and that is a sensory method. But not only that as I explained earlier but the cold sends certain signals to the brain. It's why taking ice baths is said to have so many health benefits.

Our bodies are designed to heal and I had to use that knowledge to my advantage.

But what was interesting in my therapy session was when he took me down the path of deep rooted issues I had being a single mom.

I will say that what he made me discover which was very important to be doing all of this self discovery and finding out why I spiraled so hard after the loss of Loxi, is that there were times I felt as if my only existence was to take care of my daughter. Like I wasn't good enough for anything else and I went through subconscious feelings of thinking I was being treated as if my only job and all I was good for was to provide for my daughter.

To make me happy? To make me healthy? For me to matter in this world...it simply didn't because I was only good enough to be the money machine and provider to make someone else happy.

Maybe some moms can relate, I don't know, but when you're alone, and you're a single mom and as single as it gets like me with no father involved no child support, you go through feelings of being treated as if that's the expectation. Doesn't matter if you are having a bad day or you're sick...you better still do X, Y, Z to make someone else happy, to make someone else's life comfortable.

But your comfort...doesn't matter.

That was how I felt.

It was there all along in my subconscious and I knew it was time to take care of myself because I knew at the end of the day only I could do that, only I was responsible for myself yet it was as if I was waiting for someone to come save me or take care of it all for me. I learned I couldn't rely on anyone else to do it, not even family because it's simply *not* their job.

Yes the Bible says to help your neighbor, and I should have asked for help with small things, big things...but I just didn't know how to do that. I only knew and understood how to handle every single thing alone. Which is fine if that was how I wanted to handle it but what wasn't fine was to also expect others to somehow read my mind and jump in to save me.

I looked at everyone else around me to fix me but me but it was never their responsibility. I think I thought this because I had always taken care of others so I assumed when I was down and out I needed the support.

So while you don't know it, YOU, my subscribers, were all I had. You were a major positive thing in my world.

Do you understand how crucial you became to keeping my head above water?

I wish so much I could show you into my heart so you could see. I know I didn't engage much and most times I do not with my videos in comments, but I read them and when I post I know I'm sharing something that I love with others who love it too and it makes me feel connected to you. And I needed that. You did that for me. How can I ever thank you? It's not good enough but I am truly humbled by your kindness to me.

There were days that were so good when I opened my eyes and saw you. My days were good because of you. Now I always knew you were there, I have had so much kindness from you all for so many years but it's important to understand how different I was in this time. How lost I was, how hard I was just hanging on. So my mind went through days of darkness and light. And the light was always you. I would wake up and I would think "I want to give them a good video today"
And that was how I got through it.
When January hits I'm now in this place where I am so focused on taking care of myself that now I'm really seeing the benefits of what taking care of myself looks like and I want to keep chasing this feeling.
I want to be the best version of myself that I can be. And while you did so much for me, I was still human. I still struggled being in front of the camera a lot. I was in the place where I didn't even feel good enough for you. Like I was letting you guys down by not doing my normal content and for not being my normal cookie self, but when I look back yes I was not my full self but if I didn't have you, I wouldn't have put up videos. I wouldn't have had the distraction I needed to keep my mind calm. It all worked like a very complicated puzzle piece.

So now I am FINALLY putting myself first, I am finally taking care of my body, I'm finally seeing the results of what happens when you properly care and love yourself and I want to keep this doing. I want to keep giving back to myself and that's when I think…it's time to move.

Now I'm in this "me" era which sounds selfish but I needed it and I have ZERO guilt for it, and I think to myself "you know what, I did my job as a mother putting my daughter first. I raised my daughter through high school and college and now it's time for me to live out my dream and it's ok maybe to put myself first for this one thing.

That dream? To live by the beach.

And that's when it all goes downhill.

I mean we all know the dream didn't work. I am back in Texas now, but that's what this story is about: the last two years of my life.

So the first year I lose my dog, my body falls apart, my mind leaves me and goes down into an abyss with sparks of light here and there because of you, I get another dog, I start to heal myself. I fight my way out of the darkness.

The second year….I spend getting screwed financially, missing my brother, my niece and nephew, my home town, and I start to go through another round of feeling defeated, wishing I had Loxi with me because she was my comfort.

It of course wasn't supposed to go this way. I had an idea and I most definitely fantasized on how it would go but nothing seemed to go right.

It didn't start that way, it seemed to start off strong.

Because of Covid and everyone moving to Texas and to Florida, I saw the market for my house go through the roof. It was so insane that at one point I knew I wanted to take advantage of this market and sell my house whether I ended up in Florida or not.

This is where I am going to get a little vulnerable and give numbers because in order to fully give you the effect of just how bad Florida turned out to be, I think numbers might be crucial here.

Buckle up because it will feel like a huge punch to your gut, so you can imagine how I felt because it was my money and I could have done so much with it. I could have made a million and one better choices with this money but instead, I make the worst mistake of them all.

Anyway, I knew that my neighborhood was also very hot and I know it's all in vlogs and I explained my thought process of moving but I will admit that it did feel like it happened overnight in regards to me making the decision to move out of state.

I always knew I wanted to try living in Florida, that was not an overnight thought, however, I do remember thinking "I want to move now" and by the next morning that was done and confirmed in my mind. Once I make a decision there is no stopping me, I'm trying to get better about that. Getting better about thinking things through and letting thoughts marinate lol.

So next thing I know I'm looking at houses in Florida and I wanted to live in Destin.

The thought had come to me during the family vacation prior in 2021 where it hit me like a ton of bricks.

"Why don't I just LIVE here?" I had been vacationing in Destin for over ten years at this point, I knew this town like the back of my hand and I even had a specific neighborhood I wanted to live in.

But as I looked for homes and as I spoke with my Florida realtor, I knew that finding a home in Destin was going to be extremely difficult for many reasons. Pricing and being outbid by buyers who wanted to turn the homes into Airbnbs because it is a vacation town.

And what I saw in my price point, which was still very high to be honest, I was still looking at very old and run down homes in the million dollar price range.

It just wasn't looking good.

Then my agent showed me a house in a town called Navarre. Sits between Pensacola and Destin and she made it sound like Destin was just a hop away. It was in fact not as close as I thought but it wasn't a horrible drive either. So in my head I thought ok, I can live in this smaller town and drive into Destin and shop and do all the things I love and get a really beautiful house for a better price, so I thought this was the best of both worlds.

What I end up learning is that while yes Destin was only 17 miles away it was still a longer drive because speed limits are in the 30s so it just takes forever to get to places so I end up finding myself rarely going into Destin at all.

I'm jumping ahead of myself here...let's take a step back and talk about the house she shows me.

It's the best house I have seen at this point. It's relatively new, move in ready and I wouldn't have to fix anything up.

Or so I think.

It sits on a golf course, which I actually was not a fan of. I have lived on a golf course before and I did not enjoy it, but at the time I was in this "made up my mind" mind frame and I was just too stubborn to back down.

So I put my Dallas house on the market, it sells in two days to California buyers and I make almost half a million dollars in cash on this deal.

I bought my house at $374,000 and sold it for
$822,000.

Never had I ever seen so much money in my life
sitting in my bank account.

It jumped in value in two years by half a million
dollars which is insane and also because a lot of
Californian's moved to Texas and California has a
Capital Gains law and because of this it's cheaper to
dump money into a house than to get taxed for it.

So I get my Dallas house under contract while I sign
the contract on the Florida house. It's all moving so very
fast that I don't have time to really process what I am
truly doing. I'm blinded by the money.

All of this really in weeks time from making the
decision to finding the Florida house and to putting my
house under contract. You would think my head is
spinning but really it's so distracting that I don't even get
a chance to really sit and think "should I do this?"

Because now that I know what I can sell my Dallas
house for, like I said earlier, I am going to sell it and get
this equity. I felt like it was a financially smart decision
and that is what real estate is about. Getting into the
market and selling your home for more than what you
bought it.

So I really thought I was making the right choice here.
But I didn't. OH NO. I did not.

There was a time where I was feeling little voice in
my head say:

"Can you really give this house away?"

"Can you really let someone else live in this house?"

"Someone else will own this house"

"This is your house, not theirs"

"This is their house, not yours"

And I buried all of those thoughts away. I even started to feel physically ill on closing day.

I remember driving to the title company and feeling very weird and very nervous and even though I was closing that day I would still be living in the Dallas house for a month or so because I did a lease back. Which just means I could live in the house until a certain date but while I'm living there it will legally no longer be mine. I struggled with that alone more than I can describe.

This home was my first home purchase and I felt so proud of myself and combined with how much I loved it...it was not an easy decision.

Something else kept telling me it was time to go and I really wish I hadn't listened.

And because it was a cash deal there wasn't very much paperwork to sign so it happened so quickly and once again I was left feeling weird and distracted. It wasn't until I left and drove back to the house and pulled up into the driveway and I saw the house completely different because it was no longer mine and I wasn't quite sure I did the right thing.

I looked up at that beautiful house, the house that I LOVED mowing, and planting flowers, and decorating and I can't tell you the amount of times I would just walk outside and look up at it.

I took so many pictures of that house the past two years that I owned it it's unreal.

So when I pull up and I realize it's not my house anymore, it belongs to someone else it didn't feel right. IT FELT WRONG.

But then I check my bank account and I see over $400,000 staring back at me and I'm like...well maybe it's not sooooo bad...

So I let my mind win over my heart and I push forward. They say money is the root to all evil. It's most likely true. Because no matter how much money I made on this deal, I look back now and I don't know that it was worth it.

The real problem is what I end up doing with the $400,000+ money...that's where the story gets gut wrenching.

Remember that punch to the gut I said you would get soon...yeah it's coming.

A week later I think, I end up having my closing on the Florida house. We had a mobile notary who came to my house and in that sweet little kitchen I loved so much that I had adorned beautiful seasonal decor where Mikah and I sat down and I signed my name to the Florida house.

Now the Florida market is also very hot and homes and typically very expensive in most parts of Florida. I was shocked at what you get for a million dollars there versus what a million dollars looks like in Dallas, Texas. I wanted a home that was new and was move-in ready. I did not want a DIY project and in Florida for the areas I was looking in that was extremely difficult. Because most homes are outdated and still somehow over a million dollars. The house I found was close to that number but it was fairly new, hurricane proof, and it was move-in ready. I didn't have to do one thing to it. So I settled. But of course at the time my mind didn't think so.

Instead at this point my mind is excited. I see no flaws in my plan whatsoever.

I get to finally live out my dream and live by the beach and most importantly I am finally doing something for ME.

That felt so right at the time. So right that I buried all of those wrong feelings I felt about giving my home away to someone else.

We start packing, I start the process of scheduling one of my cars to be shipped, get the movers scheduled, scheduling disconnections of the Dallas house and connections of the Florida house and it's all keeping me VERY VERY distracted from the deep love and attachment I have to that Dallas home. The home that now belongs to someone else when still in my mind even to this day it belongs to me.

It's my house, it will always suit me better than anyone else. That's what I think.

But it doesn't matter because it's not legally my home anymore.

The last night we spent in the house a huge storm came through. What is it with these storms coming into my life at pivotal moments? A sign perhaps?

It's the biggest storm to ever come through because I couldn't sleep a wink.

It's somehow symbolic or ironic that it stormed that night when the storm on Loxi's passing made me spiral. Yet this storm comes through almost as some time of reminder and I'm oblivious to everything around me. I clearly was going through it but didn't know it.

And by 4am we are up, by 5am we are loaded up in our cars and then we leave. I look at the house in my rearview mirror one last time. And it's beautiful. The white flower I newly planted that I didn't get to enjoy they are sitting there looking back at me. My beautiful pink Crepe Myrtles that I fixed from the previous owner who didn't know how to handle them and with me they flourished. They grew insanely fast in the two years I had them and I'm leaving it all behind.

Are you maybe wondering if I have driven by it now since I am back in Dallas now? Have I driven by to see it? Are my white flowers still there?How are my Crepe Myrtles doing? Do the new owners know how to properly prune them?

The answer is no.

I can't stomach seeing the house but Mikah has. She said it's pretty still but not like how we kept it.

Our house will always be pretty to me but I don't think I could ever look at it again.

I would rather look at my photos in Shutterfly and remember the memories of when it was mine, not look at it now when it's someone else's.

I don't want to taint my memories.

Who knows, maybe one day I'll drive by it and vlog it and it will be an entire experience but for now, I am not ready. I am still grieving my decisions, still battling with regret so for now it's best that I don't see it.

So on that last early morning Mikah makes a pit stop and drives by her favorite tree on our walking trail to say goodbye one final time and then from there we are gone.

Now at this point my mind knows this is it. We are going to Florida and I'm getting the beach, I'm getting a beautiful home and it's time for a new life.

PART IV

One of the biggest deciding factors I put in to leaving Dallas was I asked myself this question:

"Removing the stores/shopping, what else is keeping me in Dallas?"

The reason I asked myself this question was because that was my life at the time. All I had really going on in the majority of my personal life was shopping for the hauls of my YouTube channel.

I love my job, I have always felt so grateful to do this. There was a time where I held a full time 8-5 corporate job where I also did traveling and I was also putting out videos on YouTube and most times I was putting out videos almost daily. I was filming in bulk a lot to do this and then when I added my vlog channel I started to get very tired. I couldn't manage it all but I wanted to. I wanted to actually just do YouTube because my corporate job was becoming too stressful for me.

My job started to take advantage of me and gave me more and more duties that weren't even within my job title. I was an architect but I was asked to be an analyst as well as a project manager and while I was flattered because obviously they trusted me and I knew what I was doing, it was simply too much.

And I most certainly didn't get paid for those other roles so finally when I purchased my first home, the home that I will speak about here, the one that brought me so much joy, I finally found a reason to just make the jump, let go of my full time job and commit to YouTube.

It was one of the scariest decisions I had ever made. I have never been married before, I have never had a man pay for any of my bills, I had only ever known to support myself, so making all of these financial decisions alone but having my daughter to support I wanted to make sure I was making the best decision possible. It's why I hung onto my full time job as long as I did because I could have walked away long before that. I just wasn't brave enough to do it.

I would watch so many YouTubers (women) who would quit their jobs and commit to YouTube but they had a husband who had a full time job and I envied that so much.

They had no idea how much I wanted to be them. To be taken care of, but it simply wasn't the path I was on.

So when I finally decided I simply couldn't work myself to death I made the decision that I wanted to do YouTube.

I will never forget the first day I woke up without having to clock into my full time job.

I wish I could express to you what I felt but overall the best word that comes to mind is relief.

And pure joy.

I woke up and I was in charge of my schedule and of my day. And it felt so right for me and from that day forth I never looked back. I never once battled with wondering if I had made the right decision because I knew it was right and to this day it still feels right.

Thank you for that. Thank you for watching me, for allowing me to get to a place after so many years that I was able to turn YouTube into my full time job. I only ever got to do this because of you.

I kept my life simple and I was alone mostly so when I left my house it was to go to Dollar Tree, Homegoods, Hobby Lobby, Walmart, etc... that's it. Just shopping at stores.

I also, for the sake of making a decision just for myself, I removed family members from the equation. So obviously I knew if I moved to Florida I would be

1) leaving my hometown
2) leaving my brother his family and my uncle and his family

because I knew this decision was for being selfish and making all the best "healthy" decisions for myself I had to leave my family out of it. I was healing myself mentally and physically still at this point, so I was chasing that new life of starting to put myself first and doing all the things that just felt healthier for me. I was tired of being SICK. And I mean sick from panic, from stomach pain, from it all.

And one of the biggest factors was my cough. I touched on this several times that really I couldn't keep having this dry air/cold air induced asthma because it was taking a toll on me.

This was another health issue I faced since I was thirteen years old.

I couldn't keep coughing and coughing my life away so I attributed the Dallas air to this because when I would visit Florida guess what? No coughing because the humidity was better.

That is what my lungs needed because dry air impacted me in a way that would probably surprise people who don't realize how damaging dry air actually is.

It would wake me up out of my sleep and I would get asthma attacks, so bad that I would dry heave and sometimes even vomit from coughing so hard I couldn't breath.

Remember I'm 40 at this point and simply exhausted. Stomach issues since I was 6, lung issues since I was 13...I couldn't keep doing this garbage anymore.

I was tired. Blessed that I didn't have worse health issues, but still tired nonetheless. It's exhausting having diarrhea multiple times a week for decades upon decades. It's tiring coughing so much you pee all over yourself. Yes it's not pretty but that was my life. I was just so damn tired of it all.

Florida was the solution in my mind. Especially when I asked myself that question "Removing the stores/shopping, what else is keeping me in Dallas?"

And this was my answer to myself "nothing"

Nothing else besides the shopping was keeping me in Dallas. There was no scenery (compared to the beach) it was all just flat and boring. That's what I thought at that moment when I answered myself.

And it was good enough for me, enough validation to say my decision was the right one.

So I remember the drive to Florida very clear like it was yesterday.

I was happy. And shockingly I was calm. Like all signs pointed that this was the right decision.

We drove through a massive storm and nothing could put a damper on my mood. An eleven hour drive felt like two because I was so happy.

It wasn't until we finally made it that we pulled into the neighborhood that I started to see why buying sight unseen might not be the greatest idea on the planet.

I bought this house sight unseen but so did the California buyers on my previous home. We both bought our homes the same way where our realtors face timed us and shows us the home that way so it's not uncommon, and actually happens quite often.

It just didn't end up being a smart decision on my part. We all know the California buyers made a great decision, my house was beautiful.

All I knew about the town of Navarre, Florida was that Jaws 2 was filmed there. Beautiful beaches, highly recommend this quaint little town but it wasn't for me. I wanted to live in Destin because it had been my target all along. But I faced one major issue: I simply couldn't afford the house I wanted with my requirements and be within my price range. It just wasn't going to ever happen. I had to go a little further out of the area and even then the home in Navarre was very pricey. I ended up putting almost all of the $400,000 I had made and put it into the Florida house. YEP. That's what I did with the money.

I could keep it, maybe even retire from it and junk journal the rest of my days, but what did I do instead? I bought an overpriced home in a town I knew nothing about and didn't even suit me from day 1.

I would have known this had I flown into Florida to check this house out for myself with my own very eyes. I would have known right then and there that it wasn't the place for me.

But I didn't, I relied on my agent and I thought "how bad can it be? It's next to Destin"

Well, I'm back in Texas now so that should answer that question.

Anyway, we were driving into this town and my heart sank. There is absolutely no offense to this town and to the residents there I just knew seeing it, it wasn't for me.

Some people love New York City, some people love the rural life, some people love the small town, big town, suburbia, house boat, RV life… just because I don't like it doesn't mean it doesn't hold value. My opinion of something doesn't make it so. Doesn't make it true, better or worse. It's just my opinion and the only person who should value my opinion is myself. So just because my opinion is that this town doesn't suit me, doesn't mean it can't suit someone else.

Just because I didn't like Navarre doesn't mean Navarre isn't a wonderful place. A town like this one is the perfect combination for someone who wants a quiet, peaceful life with the beach nearby. It's quite actually a dream for most people, it just didn't end up being *my* dream.

Trust me, I wanted it to be my dream. I didn't just give up the most perfect house on the planet for nothing. I did it for the dream I had. I had so much hope, I had so much faith in it.

I gambled and I lost.

I had given up my hometown, my home of my dreams that I loved so very much, the home that held all of my last memories with Loxi, I gave it up for one word.

Hope.

I had so much hope in this dream, hope in this town, so when we finally arrived and we were driving through this town which only had one major road: 98, my heart simply sank.

Absolutely nothing besides this:

Walmart
Publix
Dollar Tree (Thank God)
Dollar General

And that's about it when it comes to shopping stores. There was no Target, no Starbucks, you can forget about HomeGoods or TJ Maxx because those weren't there either and your options to get food was also limited.

I learned just how sheltered I was living in a booming metroplex my entire life because a small little town put me in shock.

Now, most know I don't shop at Target, so I don't mention Target because I need one, I'm just showcasing that the bigger chain stores were not in this town.

I also understand life is about perspective. I realize someone reading this could think I sound ungrateful but I don't think I am. I just grew up knowing Town A and that was my bubble. So when I stepped out of my bubble into Town B, I was in culture shock.

Again nothing wrong with any of this but it was a culture shock and I was HELLA shocked.

I had moved to what felt like a rural beach town and rural locations didn't do much for me.

And you know what's crazy too (Besides me)?

The fact that all of this occurred in 2022 and there is such a thing as google earth and internet…all of this could have shown me this town and yet I never once utilized any of this to make a smart calculated decision. Instead I threw my hands up and said "yeah this is exactly what I'm going to do, what could POSSIBLY go wrong?"

I deserved everything that came to me from this decision and I know that. I wasn't trying to be dumb, I was just naive and I had faith.

Trust me, the only person I blame this on is myself. However, my Florida agent had sent me videos of what was supposed to be my "neighborhood" entrance and areas and she wasn't very truthful in her videos. I had asked her to drive around and show me what the entrance and areas looked like and she sent me a video of the bridge that led to the beach making it seem as if that was how you get to my home. It was not that way at all I would find out later.

That wasn't the only thing she did wrong... I'll get to that later as well.

So I pull up into the neighborhood and I'm very shocked and confused but I'm reminding myself this will take some getting used to because I'm so used to Dallas suburbs, because that is the life I have only ever known since I was seven years old and being in a new place will take time.

I had even said this in my past YouTube videos. I said I was already preparing myself for a change and that I knew it wouldn't be easy and I even said I knew I would eventually end up back in Texas at some point in my life and I could also end up in Texas earlier if this dream didn't pan out. I knew all of these things were a possibility.

And Toto, I wasn't in Dallas anymore.

I didn't grow up with money so my home growing up was smaller than all of my friends, our fence was falling apart and we didn't have a front door for the longest time, just some wood lumber that was screwed in and had a boarded up look. I grew up very embarrassed of my home because all of my friends were wealthy and I ıw their homes and mine just wasn't even in the same ʋallpark.

Lots of times we didn't have food in the fridge and I remember when we made the grocery trip I was so excited to stock the fridge. I would also sneak to the fridge to grab snacks and I was always caught. My grandparents were wonderful, don't get me wrong, but we still struggled a lot financially.

And being a young mom I didn't have any money in my 20s. So I went from being below average family income growing up to being even more below average raising Mikah. Times where we had no food and what food I had I gave to Mikah and I didn't eat just so she could.

This sounds so insignificant but I will never forget the day I had some money and I got to spend it on Justice clothing. Back in the early 2000's that was all the rage for girls. Now it's available at Wal-Mart, but back then it was highly sought after and I felt so proud I could get my daughter the same clothes all her wealthier friends were wearing.

There was a lot we both had to sit back and watch others around us have, but we also had more than others as well but being honest it was still always a struggle to be grateful. I was, most days for sure, but sometimes, maybe like most humans, you want what you see others have around you.

All I knew what to do was work and just work hard.

I wasn't raised with money. I worked for everything I had and I worked for every job interview, for every job. I killed myself having a full time job and doing YouTube at the same time because I was just so determined to make a better life for myself.

I had no man, no other income but my own to rely on. It wasn't easy.

And all the while raising Mikah alone and with zero in child support.

I lived paycheck to paycheck and honestly not even that. I had my next paycheck already spent. I have had my lights turned off, my water turned off, my electricity turned off and even had my car towed once. My old Ford Explorer that some of you might remember in my videos. I felt so proud of myself when I paid that car off, that's why I held onto it until I moved to Florida and was yet another loss that was hard for me because there was so much symbolism in that vehicle for me.

Tough times where I couldn't pay for it, getting it towed, taking Mikah to the first day of Kindergarten and her first day of college! I moved her to Texas Tech in that car. And paying it off after all I had been through it was one of the biggest moments in my life. So giving it away was rough for me.

Before my move to Florida I sold it to my neighbor for his elderly father to drive who wanted to fix some of the issues it had. I always planned on donating it but it had so many issues I couldn't in good conscience do that. My neighbor knew of all the issues and agreed to take it on. From what I have heard since the father loves the car and he fixed all of the problems. That makes me happy.

But this book is only about the last two years. However, I wanted to highlight what I had come from because even without having money I was still used to a suburban area of life. This little Florida town seemed actually more rural and I am not a rural kind of gal.

I'm also highlighting that I grew up in a more poor situation and I fought my way out of that. The life I live now is what I worked for on my own. And nothing was given to me.

Anyway, we pull up and I'm just telling myself there are things I will get used to and that it's to be expected that change will take time and it will be worth it because I get the beach and that's all I ever wanted.

Who remembers the vlog about the beach flies??

Yeah let's get into that one later…

So we pull up to the house and I'm very happy with the house itself and I'm feeling excited again.

We walk in and both Mikah and I are very excited, the house itself is exactly as I had been shown in pictures and FaceTime calls. I remember Mikah telling me that season 2 of Outer Banks is about to premiere and she can't wait to watch it on our back patio.

I don't remember our first night in the house but I think we slept upstairs in Mikah's room together but I remember feeling hopeful. We had so much to look forward to. And then we got lucky, our moving truck was coming a day early and I was ready to tackle decorating. Since I'm giving you guys numbers I'll go ahead and tell you that this cross country move cost me $14,000. And an extra $1000 to transport the Lexus. Yeah money just starts to go down the drain at this point. Down, down, down the money pit.

Once the movers leave the first small house catastrophe event happens. Very minor but it still felt like the beginning of the domino fall.

I'm getting stuff down around the house and of course we have the washer and dryer hooked up and that's the first thing we tackle because we need clean towels, clothes etc…so it's the first thing that gets attention from the movers. They plug me all in and get all the lines where they need to go.

And when the first wash hits the drain and spins...the house floods.

We aren't 48 hours into the house and it floods.

The movers forget to put the drain hose into the wall where the water drains out so the hose was just hanging off the back of the washing machine so when the cycle went into the drain, all of that water went everywhere. I was actually shocked at how much water came out of there. It was enough to flood the huge laundry room, the hallway, the guest bathroom and into the carpet of my craft room and guest bedroom.

And we had nothing to soak up or stop this water. We had no towels, everything was still packed and I was a mess. I had a mess to look at with no solution and it was all hitting me at that moment everything that I had just done.

I folded like a deck of cards.

Looking back at that moment I knew I was still in a very vulnerable place because one little event had me down on my knees crying. I couldn't handle very much at all at the time. Maybe that's weak of me, probably is, but I did the best I could do on that day.

Eventually I found a towel or two and I did my best to soak up the water and as time went on I put that first falling domino behind me. I spent the next few months ordering furniture and decorating the house and this was when I started to notice that I'm simply not connecting to this space. It just quite wasn't the same feeling I had with the other house. But I'm thinking maybe it's the town. Because by now I'm also realizing I have to drive almost an hour to either Destin or Pensacola to go to any shopping outlets.

Maybe a lot of people do this now but I wasn't used to that. In Dallas every few miles is some type of shopping center so it was an adjustment and I wasn't a fan of being in the car for that amount of time so I found myself rarely going to Destin or Pensacola.

I was told by my Agent that Destin was fifteen minutes away. LOL. Yeah I don't think so. It was an hour and that was in OFF SEASON.

She said this because she knew she was going to lose me if I couldn't find a home in Destin. And based on my requirements she knew I would never find the right house in Destin. I had told her upfront "do not show me any other town any other neighborhood other than the area I gave her"

And she still did it.

Now she didn't force me to buy that house, I did that all on my own. So I put that fully on myself, but she never once listened to me and she knew how important Destin was to me so she lied and said it was closer than it actually was.

She wanted this house in Navarre to grab me. And it did, based on the fact that I thought I would be fifteen minutes away from Destin. Now in theory Destin was only 17 miles away...but it took more than an hour to always get there. Traffic and very low speed limits prevented the drive to ever being fifteen minutes. And I drove during less traffic times as well, so I can't imagine what it was during rush hour or in season.

I definitely felt lied to. Because I was. But there was nothing I could do about it other than to feel angry. Angry at her and angry at myself for being naive enough to believe her. I should have done the work myself. I shouldn't have bought it sight unseen. Shoulda coulda woulda right?

During the first couple of months it was impossible to enjoy the backyard at night due to frogs.

I couldn't even open a door without one jumping on me and girl ... .I don't do frogs.

So I decided to call a company and see if I couldn't enclose the patio area. I vlogged all about this on my YouTube channel and I was excited for this project but it was going to cost me.

Thank God I didn't...because my next big money pit hits not too soon after this.

But before I experience that I experience my front yard flooding.

Which was also never disclosed to me. I had never seen photos of this and when the appraiser went out it hadn't rained so the front yard pictures were dry. But I look back now and remember during our final walk through (which was the same day we were closing on our house) my agent had dropped the ball and had to postpone it due to "flooding" . She said she couldn't drive into Navarre because of all the flooding. I know now that was also a lie, because when I started to live there and it flooded massively I saw that none of the town streets flooded at all.

She was probably busy with something else and used that as an excuse because she still showed up during the "flood" so I don't know why she couldn't drive it before but whatever.

I had asked her to show me the front yard on FaceTime on that final walk through and looking back I see she was hiding the flood on my property. Yes my property flooded but the streets did not.

My property had a dip in the front yard. It was how most of the Florida houses in this neighborhood were because it was their decision to keep the flood out of the streets but also out of the home.

I wasn't used to this system either. I didn't understand why it didn't look like how Dallas handled water movement. We had sewers on the sides of the roads where water drained into, but not Florida, not this neighborhood.

They created those dips in peoples yards and at the time of her call she showed me the house with the flooded yard behind her so I never got to see it.

I had NO CLUE my house flooded like this until I experienced it first hand.

All she wanted was the sale. She didn't give a crap about being honest.

And the irony of all of this after speaking with the city? That it wasn't my house that had the issue. It was my neighbors house two doors down.

But did he flood? Nope, did anyone else flood on my street? NOPE. Just my house.

My house was built to code because it was the newest house on the block. The other houses were older and the neighbor two doors down had a higher elevation in the pipes under their driveway. And because of this my houses flooded because water can't fight gravity. Water can't stream UP, it has to stream even or down.

So while everyone else got to walk out normally to their mailbox or walk their dogs, I couldn't.

There was no way around this flood because it flooded my front yard end to end. To get the mail I had to get into my car and Loki, well he just didn't get walks. And it took days and sometimes weeks for the flood to eventually soak into the ground.

I had to then spend several hundred dollars to get the driveway power washed because of the flooding mess leaving cakes of dirt and it ruined the epoxy of my garage as well when I would go over the water in my car and roll into the driveway.

I had to fix that too for the new owners and I have to admit I was very bitter about that.

My house was up to code the others weren't but I was the one who paid for it.

A few months later the city came out to fix it. And did they even have to touch my house to fix it? No, they had to dig into my neighbors driveway and level out the drain properly. Basically lower the drain so that the water from my end up the street could travel down the drain towards his house properly.

After that the front yard flooding finally stopped.

Yes, I realize it's just a simple front yard flood, it did make daily things harder for me and Loki and if that was the only thing I had to face then it wouldn't have been a big deal to me. It was just that one thing after another kept happening.

So you're thinking what happens next?

The garage falls on top of my car. Yep. That happens.

And after that? Flies. Flesh eating flies at the beach. Now this one is more important to note. Because remember I did all of this to live at the beach.

I get excited to go to the beach, it's probably September at this point and all the out of towners are gone, kids are in school and I'm so flipping excited to go to the beach where it's empty and I get to enjoy my "new home". So I make a morning out of it. Did I say I was excited?

Because I was excited. It made all of those other issues not hurt as much.

There is an entire vlog on this. On this day that you can watch back. The only thing that I didn't mention in this vlog was that it was when I knew I wanted to go home.

I show up with everything loaded up on my arms and I see the beach and it's beautiful. I have never seen it so empty and I was so excited.

I'm thinking "this is it. This is going to be my life from now on. I'll get to come here and heal and listen to the waves, watch the waves, read my book and just sit in peace"

Then the attack of the flies.

As I get further into the sand I start feeling bites all over my body and it's a full body attack. So much so, I think I'm being stung by bees or wasps so I drop everything and I run to the water.

I'm looking around at the few people I see and everyone looks so calm and I'm in panic mode.

"Like what the hell just happened?" And I'm still getting bit in the water!

And I see that they are horse flies.

Some guy is watching me looking around confused and he shouts to me "Yeah you have to get in the water to escape them"

So I'm like "Oh ok..."

Like this is some normal thing. I had never been to the beach in September. I had only ever visited Destin in June, July and once in early August and NEVER had I ever been bitten by anything.

So I'm just flabbergasted. I'm thinking "is a dead fish or corpse around?" Is that why the flies are here? I even thought at one point after research that I was dying. Yep...I did a google medical search and thought they were attracted to me because I had too much lactic acid in my body from cancer and that was why they wanted to eat me. But nope, after doing more extensive research I learned that these flies are normal at this time of the year on the beach. So there I am going back home and thinking "I moved here for the beach and I can't even go...to the damn beach" trust me I tried coming back so many times but each time I was attacked by the flies.

It was the only thing that I liked about the town…so when that wasn't something I could enjoy I felt very sad. Very defeated and floods of regret entered my life.

That's when I decided to go back home. But that's not where the money pit issues end on the house. They only get worse.

The first thing that happens is the house almost blows up from the landscape water pump.

I had hired a company to spray my house for weeds and take care of the grass. One thing about me is I love landscape and I love curb appeal. Plus curb appeal only adds value to your home and to other's homes as well so I have always been obsessed with keeping my house looking maintained. Probably also stems from my childhood. We were the house that never mowed our lawn, never trimmed our bushes and I was embarrassed by it. One time as a child I remember trying to trim our bushes and I was stung by a bee.

Anyway it's always been this thing that I have been obsessed with so I wanted to make sure this Florida grass was kept nice. Well not only did they end up killing several of my bushes, grass, and trees…that never came back from their weed killer spray, but my lawn guys had also made changes to my water schedule.

It was all part of the conversation they had told me they made changes to it and wanted to water it certain times and days but what they did was they turned a zone on that wasn't an actual zone. My lawn only had five total zones, only five areas of sprinkler systems. But the control panel had options for several more zones. So they added a 6th zone that my underground never had…and because of this whenever the sprinkler system hit the 6th zone and water was trying to push out but there was no actual 6th zone…the water pump temperature skyrocketed.

To the point where it was steaming. Steam was coming off of it and it melted off all the sealant and if it had been running any longer than it did, I don't know what could have happened.

Thank God this 6th zone time was around 7 am. The other zone 1 started around 4 am. And it took almost three hours to go through Zone 1, 2, 3, 4, and 6 before it got to the 6th zone and the water again is trying to give the water to that zone but there are no sprinkles for this water to come out at so the water pump kept going and gone and it heated to an insane temp in which I caught because I could see the steam one morning through my craft room window. Even though this water pump was ten feet away, that was how much steam was coming out.

I ran out and saw it and turned the sprinkler off.

I had to call a repair company to come fix the damage that was made by the previous company.

It cost a lot. I cried. A lot.

This wasn't my first rodeo of dealing with men and getting screwed on situations like this because they bank on the fact that as a woman you won't know if they are lying or not.

I also fired the previous landscape company and I maintained my grass myself.

Then came the AC.

Long story short, the AC simply wasn't strong enough to handle the square footage of this home and I also had to pay a lot of money to have it fixed and properly tuned. The first guy didn't fix it properly and only messed things up more and I had to spend more money for someone else to fix it. So I'm seeing a pattern. That anyone touching my home seems to mess it up. Oddly enough I had a friend who had lived in Florida before and told me that their experience was the same.

That any work done was always messed up. Not saying this is a typical standard Florida thing. I'm sure there are good companies and good workers but it wasn't my personal experience. The last issue put me over the damn edge. It cost me eight thousand dollars.

One night I'm in my room and suddenly I hear a loud beeping sound. It sounds like it's coming from my neighbors house and it keeps going. So I get up and I walk to the side of the house to see that it's actually coming from my house.

A red light is on some box on the side of the house where the noise is coming from. So I go over to it not knowing what this box is and I'm panicked because it's late at night, I don't know what to do, so I put my hand over what looks like the speaker of where this sound is coming from and it muffles the sound a lot. So I decide to get electric tape and I tape it up to mask the sound because I know the neighbor's window directly across is his daughters room and I don't want to keep her up.

So I put tape over it, you can barely hear it and I know I will figure it out in the morning. The next day I go over to the box and I call the number that is on it.

They basically tell me that I have to call a plumber.

I still have no clue why this box has ANYTHING to do with plumbing. But ok, I'll call a plumber.

At this point I'm scared to have anyone come to my house and touch anything. Guess what happens? Yep they also mess it up, but let's get into the details of this one.

Because if I could I would sue this company. The guy on the phone, not the plumber, but the company that installs these boxes, is so helpful and actually walks me through troubleshooting this sound. There is actually a switch that you can turn this off. But the switch wasn't working. So he said that most likely it was just a fault in the electrical wiring. That the wiring was bad and triggered this alarm to go off.

Now what was this alarm for? Apparently a damn septic tank that I had NO CLUE I HAD.

We don't have septic tanks in the Dallas suburbs. We have city sewer systems.

I don't have to worry about where my shower drains to or what happens to the toilet once I flush it. Nope, never had to know where the hell any of that goes until I moved to Florida into a neighborhood where you had to have your own septic tank.

At this point I'm feeling like the tiger lady from Baby Boom. IF ONE MORE DAMN THING HAPPENS in this house I'm going to scream.

Anyway this alarm is built to trigger in the event your pump stops grinding properly and your septic tank overflows and it triggers the alarm so you know it needs attention and to NOT flush anything to not shower, to not do the dishes or laundry because that water will back up into your house. I couldn't have that!

But when the plumbing guy shows up, and at this point I'm watching his every move because I don't trust anyone in Florida at this point, and when he opens the lid to the tank it's not overfilled at all.

It's actually in proper condition. So we confirm that it is actually a bad wire that simply triggered the alarm.

There are two floaties in the tank once those floats move up in any way that will trigger the alarm. But that didn't happen because the tank wasn't overfilled. So he replaced the bad wire and then this guy had the balls to speak condensing to me about flushing tampons and how he had to clean that out. Well fun fact but Mikah and I don't use tampons so I knew it wasn't me but the previous owners. And he talked about wipes too and I figured once again the previous owners because they had just had a baby.

And I'm grinding my teeth looking at this guy who is talking to me like I'm some disgusting female for flushing that and I'm stupid for flushing that. But I keep my mouth shut.

He finishes his work, the alarm stops going off and he leaves.

Cost me several hundred dollars for this.

But do you think that is all that happened? Nope.

I start hearing my toilets make a weird gurgling noise when I flush and then doesn't flush at all.

So I call the company back and they come to take a look at it and guess what they say? ONE DAY LATER.

"Your grinder pump is broken"

And I said well you better fix it for free because my grinder pump was JUST FINE before the guy who was here touched it. He actually said it was fine and that he cleaned out all of those "products" so he must have either purposely ruined it or he did it by accident. Either way it's not a damn coincidence that my grinder pump broke less than twenty fours after you touched it. The issue wasn't the grinder pump, it was the electrical wire. However, the electrical wire hooks up the grinder pump so he had to touch it and whatever he did he didn't do it right. I called another company because I didn't trust them and I had another company come out and when they opened up the tank (this is the best way I can describe it).

And I was standing there the entire time once again. The guy simply opened the lid and looked down and he saw what ruined the grinder pump. Apparently there is a valve that turns the water back on to flow and you turn this valve off when you are working down there.

So the first guy, the jerk, turned off the valve to work but he never TURNED IT BACK ON, and that made the grinder pump basically short circuit and killed it. We took a picture of this and they advised that I call the original company back and make them pay for it. I did while these guys were at my house. I passed the phone to them because they happened to know each other. The man we spoke to wasn't the jerk though, it was the manager.

And the new company and this manager happened to be friends.

And he told him "hey man, listen your guy didn't turn the valve back on" And apparently this was enough for the manager to realize "damn, ok, we will replace this grinder pump for free"

Sounds good right? No big deal, they are going to fix it for free because they messed up but guess what the manager did a few days later? He called me and said "well I have thought about it some more and it couldn't have been the valve because something to do with water running" Even though we clearly saw the valve wasn't on.

This decent company ended up replacing the grinder pump and billed the other company for it. But it took several days for this.

Mikah and I don't have a shower to use, we can't flush the toilets but we are peeing in them. Doesn't sound great but where were we supposed to go?

We are going days without any water whatsoever for this guy to tell me he isn't responsible. I argued and argued and he said he wasn't going to pay the decent company back. I had to come out of pocket eight thousand dollars to replace this grinder pump. All of this because of the alarm and simple electrical wire turned into a nightmare. And once again yet another experience of having someone touch my house and ruin it and I am the one coming out of pocket to fix it.

I couldn't do it anymore.

I wanted to. I knew I was going to be judged by my haters, I knew what people would think but I didn't care. I couldn't live there anymore.

I wasn't happy.

I wanted to be, trust me but unfortunately I gambled and lost. Nothing in life is a guarantee; I learned that lesson quickly.

But with this house I just felt like I was always paying for someone else's mistakes.

The movers with the drain hose
The yard flooding due to the neighbors house
The repair of the new water pump
The grinder pump fiasco
The property line drama.

That was another one. The property line drama… in my neighborhood there were quite a few empty lots, on each of these lots are filled with massive tall pine trees and bushes and God knows what else, so when someone acquires a lot there has to be a clearing process of all of these things.

The owner before me, when he chose the lot the house now sits on, there was also another vacant lot next to it. So when they cleared the lot for the Florida house and the owner put up the fence (most of you have seen this fence in my vlogs where Loki plays) well that fence line he placed happened to be placed right on the other lot property line.

So when a new builder came in and cleared that empty lot next to my house and started to build a house on this property, I was approached about how my fence line was on their property.

sighs because of course it's now MY problem.

Did I place the fence there? No.

Was it my responsibility now? Yep.

Once again someone else's doing but my problem.

Y'all...when I tell you I felt as if I was in the damn twilight zone...every time I turned around there was some issue that wasn't my doing but I had to fix.

I truly felt flabbergasted by it all because I had never experienced anything like this. This is my second time owning a home and let me tell you, home ownership is not for the weak.

So I told this builder that I didn't place that fence line there and it's only about an inch on their property line and was it ok to leave it as is? Nope. Did I have to have someone come move the fence by an inch and pay more money that I care to disclose? YES I had to do that.

All I kept thinking was, ok what's next?

I am not connected with this house, my agent lied, my house was the money pit, I couldn't go to the beach, I was sitting in this house feeling like a prisoner.

That's when I know it's time to come home.

PART V

Why was I paying for everyone else's mistakes? It was as if God said "Ok you wanted this dream but it's not the plan so time to go back where I need you to be so I'm going to throw every curveball I can at you"

It just felt like one violent shove after another.

Looking back now it feels clear as day that I simply was not meant to be there but I can't help but wonder if that was the case and God was showing me my way back home why did he have me go through all of this?

Is it because we have free will and it was my decision at the end of the day to do this so this was how I had to learn that Florida wasn't for me?

ıt if we have free will sometimes I wonder why it ᴊᴄɪns as if some other force was in play here trying to show me that Florida wasn't the right path? I get very confused by this sometimes with my relationship with Him and still something I'm trying to iron out and understand.

I am very grateful I have free will and the right to choose what I do with my life but I also trust in Him so much. He clearly knows what is best for me so sometimes I can't help but ask him "Why did you let me do all that?" LOL.

I guess if it was perfect I'd be in heaven. There is a lot I don't understand and I know I probably never will but I feel confident now knowing I don't need to know or fully understand everything.

I'm ok with realizing my human brain can only comprehend so much and if I just don't get it, then I don't get it.

I'm the type of person where home is extremely important to me. It's my safe haven and it's what gives me so much of my joy.

My sister in law, who is probably the sweetest soul I have ever met, she is the cutest and most social butterfly I have ever known. She thrives on all of her relationships with each of her friends and let me tell you, the girl's got a ton of friends! She nourishes all of them, they all love her to death and she is always planning something. Always going to a birthday party, wedding, or dinner and just hearing about it exhausts me because I'm the type of person where that is more draining to me than giving me life.

But see for her and her personality it gives her a boost and does the complete opposite to me.

She isn't wrong for her life and neither am I. It's just how we are each individually wired so while some might look at my life and think "that sounds depressing" I actually enjoy my home and can't seem to get enough of my daily homebody routine. I eat it up!

It is what fuels me, so when I moved into this Florida home, gorgeous property, beautiful home, it unfortunately did nothing for me. I felt absolutely no connection to this property.

When I bought my first house, the one I sold to purchase the Florida home, I remember the first time I saw it and let me tell you it was the craziest, weirdest out of body experience I have ever had.

I remember walking into it with my agent at the time and it was fully empty and I came to a complete stop.

I then went into a range of emotions with milliseconds. Relief, confusion, awareness...

I had felt as if I had already lived in this house and that is the only way I can describe this feeling.

I walked in and it was as if in another lifetime I had already experienced living there. It felt familiar and I even had a flash of living there with all of my furniture. Sounds insane probably but it was a "whoa" moment.

And that was when I knew it was my house. I didn't look at any others.

With the Florida house I bought it sight unseen and had only experienced seeing it the first time through a phone call, so when I showed up it just felt like a house.

Nothing wrong with that, it might not be something other people care to experience, but it just felt cold to me.

Like me and this house didn't mesh.

And trust me I tried.

I would wake up and push myself, push my mind to thinking positive. I created my new little routine, get up make a pot of coffee I wouldn't drink but I loved how it made the house smell, I would take Loki or his walk and start laundry and get all the tv's dialed into the shows I wanted to hear.

But no matter how hard I tried there was only one room in that entire house I could stand and that was my office.

I never felt cozy or comfortable in my living room and my bedroom sometimes made me feel worse. I stayed out of my bedroom for as long as possible.I don't know why this is a thing for me and it makes me sometimes think I'm overly complicated for having such a quiet life but I just couldn't connect with this house. I didn't want to decorate it, I didn't love being in it, and I left it as much as I possibly could. That was when I knew there was no way I was going to overcome this.

It doesn't feel great to have spent so much money to realize a few months in "oh this isn't going to work" I didn't like having to admit that to myself let alone to others.

But it's simply what happened.

Here is what I know to be my biggest law I have for myself. Despite regrets, despite how hard something is, I will always do everything in my power to seek happiness. I wasn't going to just sit and live in this house (God willing) because I was afraid of what others would think.

If I wasn't happy then I was going to do what I could to change that. And by the grace of God I had the opportunity to come back home. I thought about every avenue before I made this decision because obviously I didn't want to find myself in yet another failed attempt. I thought, maybe I should buy a different house in a different part of Florida I could afford. I knew I didn't want to live in this town, I needed something with more people and faster paced and I knew I couldn't afford to live in Destin.

I had considered maybe moving to Pensacola but that would put me even further from Destin and this entire process was so I could be close to Destin. The place where my heart felt the most peace. I tried. I can say without regret that I'm proud of myself for trying and all alone from a financial standpoint. But it's only September at this point. I have only been living there for FOUR MONTHS. All of this happening in four months.

I didn't mention the other little issues like my insurance and the water heater in the garage with a bracket…yeah that was another plumber call for several hundred dollars, then I get a surprise bill in the mail for almost four hundred dollars for a termite inspection or repair of some sort and I'm like "what the hell is this bill?"

I'm thinking this must be a mistake so I call. Now this bill actually happened almost a year into living in Florida.

I got this bill sometime around February of this year to find out that my agent scheduled this at the time of closing and NEVER once mentioned this to me or anyone else. I never got a copy of this report, it was never disclosed on my closing documents and I was expected to pay for it.

I argued with this company that legally I had no knowledge of this that they needed to provide proof that I signed a document stating that I agreed to this inspection which of course they couldn't produce because I never signed such an acknowledgment and they had it on record that my agent ordered it. So I contacted her in which she ignored my calls and I left her an email telling her to pay for this and did she? Nope. Who did? Me.

I was just so damn tired. I felt frustrated with life. I wanted to do one thing for myself.

That's all. One thing where I wanted to live out my dream of living in a beach town and I couldn't even have that.

I just felt so sorry for myself. It's not an attractive quality I know, but I felt it nonetheless.

But you think that is where all the bad stuff stops? Nope.

It's September and It's been only four months and I'm like "oh no, bad mistake. Let's go Home." But I'm also thinking I just moved here. It was exhausting to do it and expensive as hell so why not build a house and by the time it's done it will be a good time to move back.

So that's what I do.

I end up contacting a home builder back in my favorite town, and one thing leads to another and I put down $20,000 in earnest money. It's so high with builders because what happens is people will select things like purple tile and weird paint colors and then if they drop out of the deal it's a house harder to sell with those options they put into the home. So if you back out of the deal the builder has your earnest money that they can use to change the home interior in case it's not as sellable.

At this point I have almost run out of money just like Tiger Lady from Baby Boom. I'm struggling to film on YouTube, I am struggling to decorate because I'm simply so tired so even my job is suffering a little bit. My only silver lining is the $400,000 I put into the house that if I can sell the house for what I bought it for, I will get all that money back.

Is that what happens? Laugh out loud.

Of course not.

Of course that is NOT what happens.

I put that earnest money down, Mikah and I spent several design sessions with the interior designer and we picked out our entire house. It kept me sane.

That was why I traveled back to Texas so much to see the progress of the house.

I finally felt like I understood the lesson I needed to learn.

I learned what home meant to me. What TEXAS meant to me. I learned that I was just always thinking the grass was greener and it wasn't. I learned where I wanted to settle. Yes it wouldn't change the dry air situation and I would have to deal with that but I also learned it was time to take care of my health properly and that if I managed my humidity the right way with my lungs I could live at home and no cough up my lungs and change my underwear so many damn times from peeing from each cough.

Sounds silly but when you cough like that and it's hard for most of your life, it's tiring.

Imagine having a cough for months at a time? It takes a toll on your lungs and your stomach muscles and coughing after Covid? Don't do it in public. People look at you like you are carrying a disease. I used to cough so much I couldn't even go to a movie theater.

Anyway, by December I reached out to a mortgage company and got myself a loan officer and told him what kind of loan I wanted.

Being self employed I prefer Bank Statement loans, they are simply the easiest so he knew all along that was the loan type and he knew the purchase of my construction loan would be contingent upon selling my Florida home.

And I would put the Florida home up on the market in January. I find a real estate agent and she comes over to meet me and brings me the neighborhood and data and several listing numbers that she determined would all be good numbers to list my house at. We sit at the kitchen table and I tell her after she shows me the neighborhood comps and the four numbers she presents to me as the list price and I tell her that the most important thing to me isn't the list number. It's that we sell the house as quickly as we can because I can't afford to lose my construction house. I tell her exactly when this construction house is supposed to be completed so the house MUST sell prior to June of 2023.

She advises that January is a good time to list and then asks me what number I want to list my house at. At the time in December my house was worth more than what I had bought it at.

Or so the market said.

So I pick the middle numbers she gives me. Not the highest and not the lowest and she says that the number will guarantee a buyer because my house is one of the best homes in the neighborhood with one of the best golf course lots if not the best. I sign with her, we get the photos taken and come January 1 the house is listed.

And what happens?

Nothing. Crickets.

Between January and March I had maybe four showings. Four.

Meanwhile I'm confused. She just says that this is the market is but I'm not buying it. I think it's the number. I think she gave me bad numbers.

And when I think back to when I bought the house my agent at the time said that the current owner had received several low ball offers. And I gave him asking price so I shouldn't be surprised by this in the slightest. I learned that my house can be worth one price but that doesn't mean a buyer is willing to pay for it. And in this case, no one in this town saw that this house was worth what the market was actually suggesting that it was worth. I think that if this house was located in Destin or Pensacola it would have sold for what I paid for it and actually maybe even way more.

But it simply wasn't worth what the market said it was worth in this town.

And that was my mistake.

I shouldn't have given him asking price.

But regardless I had an appraisal done and the appraisal at that time came in right at the asking price, it made me learn that the housing market is actually very crazy and it felt like a roller coaster ride straight into the pits of hell.

So how the heck does my house lose so much value in under a year? In just six short months?

There I am, upset because I told her during our first meeting that the number needed to match a quick sell while also being good enough to stick to because what I didn't want to do was lower the price. I think once you lower the price, which is public data, then it only opens up for potential buyers to give you an even further low ball offer. Buyer sees a house sitting on the market, they see the price has been lowered and naturally what are you going to do? Hmmm maybe they are desperate to sell it, let me give them an even lower offer.

So I wanted a number that we felt confident in that we didn't have to change.

Now I do realize that sometimes you have to go with the market. I know that, but her number was so far off that it actually ended up being the very reason why I lost the construction home.

It was simply too high from the start and because of that took way too long to sell.

The agent didn't understand the market and didn't understand the town and town's median income and that the price of my home was simply too high and would only appeal to out of towners wanting to move south.

My house ended up selling for two hundred thousand LESS than what we had started with. My house ended up competing with other homes that were less than in square footage, older homes that needed a lot of work and didn't have a land lot as gorgeous as mine. I all but gave that house away. Congrats to the new owners who got it at that low low price not to mention that this town is on the path to boom up like Destin. So in a few short years that home will be worth so much and those new owners will get all that equity that I can't help but think belongs to me LOL.

So every time we lowered that price, I lost more and more of that $400,000 I put in.

And as we got to May and no buyers, and then finally June I got two bites. And they wanted the house for two hundred and fifty thousand less than what I was willing to give.

But at this point, I was done. I was so exhausted and I couldn't understand why I bought it for such a high price when all along it was never worth that.

The comps in the neighborhood were all almost three hundred thousand less than what I bought. How could my house be so expensive above all the others?

At this point I know that out of the $400,000 I lost $250,000. I only now had $150,000 which yes still a lot of money only problem was the price of the construction home was based off of me thinking I was going to get $400,000.

It was my money that I had made on my previous home. And I lost it to Florida.

But I could still make the deal work with getting out $150,000 or so I thought.

But then came the inspection.

Good God, the inspection.

This house was mint. When I had my inspection done, just the year before nothing major came back. The only item that came back on my inspection was a little caulking that needed to be done in the master bathroom but that is the most minor item and not required to even be repaired.

So I'm thinking ok, now it's my turn to sell this house and when these buyers do the inspection this house should come back solid with no issues right? I mean, nothing had happened in the one year we lived there, so I shouldn't have anything to worry about.

OH NO.

That would have been way too easy.

So what comes back on the inspection report?

The balcony (out of my Mikah's room) had wood rot...hmmm interesting. How does wood rot to a point that needs repair from under one year? Not to mention we never really stepped foot out there at all. I know I never went out there and Mikah didn't either because of the bugs, so how did that happen in one year?

A leak in the garage sink, several shingles on the room needed to be repaired, the fireplace had to be cleaned out, and the inspector also came back and said that we had mold in the upstairs room.When I heard about the mold I lost it. I thought, well there goes this deal, when someone hears about mold you can forget it.

I'm on the phone with my agent while she is telling me this and she says there is a black mark on the ceiling of Mikah's room and I happen to say this outloud (I'm in the airbnb in Texas at this point) so I can't see this mark she is referring to. And thank God I said this outloud, because if I hadn't repeated what she said to me, it would have cost me so much money because she was advising that we were going to have to have someone cut into this ceiling to see where the mold was coming from.

The reason why I am so thankful I repeat this outloud is because Mikah hears me say "a black mark on the ceiling of the media room? I have never seen a black mark or mold in the house"

And Mikah is walking by and ya'll….this is what she says.

"Oh that's not mold, that's when I lit the ceiling on fire because I was trying to kill a bug"

LMAOOOOO!!!

Lord, Jesus, I can't.

Me and my agent laughed so hard and let me tell you how relieved I was to know it was simply black from the flame of her match. That is an easy fix. Just wiping down the ceiling and slapping some good old paint on it, clearly much better than having to cut a hole into the ceiling to find mold that never existed all because my daughter thought let me instead kill this bug with a flame instead of like, I don't know, with a shoe or something.

All I can say is thank God the house didn't catch on fire.

At this point though if it had I don't think I would have been the slightest surprised by it. Isn't this story just a nightmare?

I finally pack up all my stuff and this time I sell everything.

This time I know I can't afford to spend $15,000 in moving costs. And I don't want to. I get pods instead and I sell everything but my couch, my washer and dryer and of course all my holiday decor.

I still spend around $6000 in moving pods.

I don't even care anymore at this point to let go of all of my things I love so much because I'm so mentally exhausted. I'm just happy that this house is selling at this point that I'm willing to let go of things that I'm emotionally tied to..

I sold my Dallas home in a matter of days and to move to Florida and get hit with the reality that this home won't sell fast because the household median income caters to a different price range, selling my home was going to be tougher. As a matter of fact everyone that walked my home were coming from other states.

This little town just had a harder market.

And I should have known that. I should have been adult enough, smart enough to think about this before I had bought that house.

But when I saw that house I thought wow look how fast my Dallas home sold for, and look how beautiful this Florida house is, surely it will sell just as quickly.

Nope. Took six months. Half a year to sell my house, and going from selling my first home in a few short days to half a year, it was a shock to me. I wasn't a real estate professional, that is why I hired one because I didn't know too much about it so when I would ask my agent what was happening and why my house was selling I didn't not like hearing "I'm not sure, I'm just as confused as you are"

WHAT?

What do you mean you don't know?

That didn't feel good to hear at all. I felt once again burned by Florida. And I know it has nothing to do with Florida. Florida was great, the people living in Navarre were wonderful. They were kind and sweet and I loved all of my neighbors, I just truly felt as if Florida just didn't seem to suit me and that came as a surprise to me.

Not to mention that the air seemed even drier which surprised me. I woke up more nights than I can count waking up into a coughing fit from how dry my throat was. Times where I felt as if I could breath because the air was so dry. I had to sleep with a humidifier spraying directly into my face which soaked my sheets by the time I woke up in the morning. So the biggest reason for moving didn't help me at all. I had no idea why I stopped coughing when we would go on our family trips to Destin but the air in my house was very very dry.

And in those six months while the house was up for sale I was holding my breath and praying every time I had a showing that this was going to be the one. The buyer who would give me an offer only to feel disappointment time after time when I got the feedback that the house was too expensive even though data still showed my house was worth the asking price.

I cried a lot.
I felt as if I was being punished.

I was afraid something else would happen to the house and it would be more money down the drain, I was afraid a hurricane would come through and ruin the house and then I would be stuck with it forever, I was afraid I would never make it back home.

And there I was yet again. Holding in the stress. And then it hits me. This is how I have always been. I have always handled stress poorly. That is why it's so hard not to let it affect me but it doesn't mean I can't change that about myself. It's never too late to want to do better, be better, because you are so truly important. And it's not selfish to love yourself, to take care of yourself, to treat yourself before others. It's important because I think it's my responsibility to take care of myself and no one else's but I also think even during hard times I need to remember to be a good "neighbor" as God instructed in the Bible. I always thought God meant this term literally. Like all I have to do is help my literal next door neighbor but I realize now lol that he meant to those around you in your community. It's something that I love doing when I'm doing great in life but when I fall under stress I'm more cranky. I'm not as forgiving or kind and I think the lesson for me was to always be a good neighbor no matter what I'm going through. I'm only human, it's still something I work on every single day and I will fail here and there but I want to always remember to do the very best I can.

I literally went into the most negative frame of mind after I had done all that work to heal myself. I didn't just change my food, I changed my thought process. I knew I had to get out of my mental slump and to do that I had to be kinder to myself, I had to speak better of myself, I had to think positive thoughts of myself, the world, and others around me because sitting in my negative thoughts only impacted me harmfully.

A scientist once did a study with two glasses of water. One glass he spoke to it out loud, he was kind to it, encouraging and positive. While the other glass of water he was negative and put it down time after time after time. After this he took both waters and put them in the freezer. Once the water was frozen he extracted it from the freezer to find that each cup had frozen differently.

The glass he was kind to the ice was clear, smooth. Like clean ice on a skating rink. The other glass however, the one he spoke negatively to was frozen in a foggy state with many cracked lines.

His thesis was to prove that water holds memory and energy. And that positives and negatives will have separate experiences. I believe that. I believe that being positive is healthier on a human's body, while negative has more impact that most people know.

I also learned that another study was done, not sure by who, perhaps Harvard but I can't quote this, that your body doesn't know the difference between different traumas. For example you could have been in a car accident and lost an arm or you could have lost your pet but your body doesn't know the difference between physical and emotional trauma. One can still be greater than the other but it doesn't automatically mean that physical trauma trumps emotional trauma. It really depends on the human and how they handle certain things. For some the trauma could be greater to lose a pet than to lose an arm to the body. It's all about how you internalize the stress.

So I knew that if I kept this up and held all of this stress, all of this regret and worry I was only going to damage myself further. And I have to tell you I failed.

I tried so hard. I tried to be positive, I tried to think only the best thoughts but Florida got the best of me. I hate to admit it but I lost that one. I battled with so many different emotions but mainly I was angry with myself. Anger, regret...

I know now that this all happened for a reason but at the time I couldn't understand.

I had been a tired single mom, I had raised my daughter, survived high school and college and now it was my turn. And my turn felt like a slap in the face... I struggled with that a lot.

I found it harder to stay in the house during these six months while the house was up for sale. I felt like I was suffocating so I left as often as I could by taking several walks a day. I for sure thought that my neighbors probably thought I was weird. And most times if they looked closely they would find me walking with a tear stained face.

My routine was get up, go to Dollar Tree, come home, film my videos, do yard work, go for a walk with Loki, take him back, go for a run, come back and walk Loki again. Take yet another walk, then load up Loki into the car and take him for a nightly car ride. And then sleep.

I did that on repeat over and over. I was in survival mode for sure and I had to keep my mind occupied but it was almost impossibe. Every single day it was constant thoughts of the house selling.

I guess I'm just not as put together as I thought I was. Maybe I am just going through a pocket in my life where I'm struggling with my decisions and I'm struggling with how I choose to react to those decisions. I know I'm doing the best I can in those moments. It might not be the best I have done before, but it's the best I can do right now. And maybe that's life. It's just doing the best with what you got. And I do have it made. I'm talking about hundreds of thousands of dollars that I know a lot of people do not have and I'm lucky to get what I was able to get from selling the Florida house but it's still a punch to the gut to lose $250,000. It's hard knowing I had a lot of that money and I lost it. I lost it due to the hard market in this little beach town.

I learned a lot about buying and selling. I will tell you that. I will know a lot more when I get into this market again.

Eventually I did get an offer. But before they could even put their earnest money down, even though I asked my agent over and over that the earnest money hasn't been turned in by them and that this isn't how it's done and I was right, these buyers pulled from the deal at the last minute. And because they never submitted their earnest money I didn't get to keep it. That is what earnest money is for those that might not know what it truly means. In the simplest of words, earnest money is to show your seriousness and so you don't waste people's time. They wasted my time, and I got nothing from it. When you go under contract you can no longer legally show your home to others. So that is what earnest money is for. So you don't waste the seller's time. It makes buyers more accountable to keeping their word because who wants to lose several thousands of dollars?

Well these people got under contract, I had to stop showing my home and I never got the earnest money when they backed out. So back on the market it went and luckily I had another offer. It was low. I was tired so I took it.

I packed up, Mikah and I loaded up our cars and we finally drove home even though the house hadn't closed yet. At this point I thought if these buyers backed out I will just keep the house up for sale while I rent and wait until the house does sell. If that means I have to lose the construction home then I have to lose it but I couldn't live in Florida anymore. I was mentally whipped.

And please understand I'm not just mentally whipped from all the house issues, but I'm mentally whipped with myself. I'm even sick of my own shit.

But luckily these buyers held on, however I got one final blow…and this is what unfortunately killed my construction home. The appraisal came in on the Florida house and it was $30,000 too short.

I had my clear to close on my construction house, I was ready to go, I just needed to close on the Florida house and then I could turn around and close on my new house but the appraisal came in too short.

I had to sell my Florida home for a certain number to make the construction house numbers work. I needed to get the equity that I had put into the Florida house but the appraiser was not kind to me.

And within days of closing on my construction home, the one I spent a year working on and watching all of my design selections come to life… I lost over $30,000. I was so close.

I could have stil done the deal but I was so afraid of putting in all the money I had left into the new house, it felt as if I was going to repeat the same mistake twice and I couldn't get myself to clear out my bank account that much.

Had I gotten the $400,000 I would be sitting in that house right now with no worries and extra money in my pocket. My original plan when I thought I was selling it for the price I paid for it, I was going to use that money to spend some time to finally become a writer. To achieve my ultimate dream of creating romance stories. That plan quickly went out the window.

The Florida market laughed at me, took my money, and I lost my dream home. So I had to just let it go. It was the final devastating blow from Florida.

How could a dream turn into a nightmare?

What had I done to deserve that? That is what I thought. More pity party for me.

I realize I lost sight of being grateful for what truly mattered. My health.

Mikah's health. That is where true wealth lies. I understand that of course and I have been so very grateful for my new found health and my peaceful stomach but that also doesn't mean that things like this aren't hard to process. It doesn't mean just because I have my health I can't cry a little over how crappy my decision was. I gambled and I lost.

But here is the biggest thing I learned. God never left my side.

That is what he wanted me to see, to learn. I had super high moments in my life and I have had bottom of the barrel moments in my life and both he was with me. I have been through a lot more than just what you are reading, especially as a child. Things I will never disclose. But I learned He has always loved me so much and He has always been with me. I lost sight of Him, but he never lost sight of me. I may not understand why I had to learn the lesson the hard way but I learned more about myself and for that I am grateful.

I learned that I belong in Texas and not because Florida did me dirty, no I realized I belonged in Texas because I missed home and I had taken it for granted. I was simply stuck in a rut and I thought the solution was to leave it but I know now that wasn't the right solution. The right thing was to fix myself because no matter where I was in the country I was always going to be running thinking I wanted something else when really the root of the issue was me. I learned to be grateful and live in the moment instead of always trying to jump to the next.

I learned that even home or the most beautiful beaches weren't going to make my life better because the problem wasn't where I lived but how I saw the world.

And the problem was that I was stuck in a rut and didn't see that. Now I do love my routines and I will always continue those but I think what I was missing was more friends. Something to do, a time to get dressed up and just go out on the town. To live life a little more out of my house.

Nothing wrong with sitting at home all the time, especially during these weird times with everything going on in the world and I will most certainly always be a homebody, but when I started to see the comparison between Dallas and Navarre...they are just two completely different experiences and I had taken Dallas for granted.

I missed all the people, the population of a massive metroplex, I missed the faster pace of life, I missed having an NBA team, and what do you know, I missed the shopping stores too. The irony is that it was the question I left out to make my decision in my move and it turned out to be more important in my life than I thought.

Perhaps pathetic to some, but this is my life and it's all I know.

It was simply too big of an adjustment to go from one extreme to another but there are times where I know that had I moved to Destin I might not have had such a hard transition and I probably would not have come home.

Destin is a full town with lots of people, a bustling city with shops and laughter and I still love it as much as I did before.

It really came down to Navarre was simply too rural for me and my soul just didn't thrive. I wish it had, I truly do.

I have met so many of you actually in Navarre which surprised me considering how small this town was but know that I love you all and I love your little town and thank you for welcoming me in. I wanted it to work so much but you can take the girl out of Texas but you can't take the Texas out of the girl. When I did go into Destin I had the best days, so I know I was on the right track when I thought moving to Florida would make me happy, but at the end of the day I couldn't afford to live there. When I drove in and went to my little breakfast spot and had my cinnamon roll and freshly squeezed orange juice seeing the beach on the other side of the road…that was the good life for me.

But I wanted to experience that daily. I couldn't it was just too far and it took time away from Loki and it just well…it just didn't work out. I was in Texas, fully moved back recently in an AIRBNB when I learned that while the new buyers would get to capitalize on an amazing deal on this Florida house because it was stunning, I would lose my dream home.

It was a huge blow. I just kept losing.

And this deal was actually killed because of my loan officer. At the time of selecting the Bank Statement program I did not know about the 20% down requirement.

When I found out how much money I was losing on the Florida house I reached out to him and said hey, I'm going to need more loan amount can you raise it?

And he said yes, are you ok with me pulling your credit? Because this was still a few months before my own closing. So I gave him the go ahead at the time. But then when my clear to close came in and I saw the bottom line of what I was supposed to bring I asked him why my loan amount wasn't going up and he said because the I had to bring 20% of my purchase price.

?!

Then why did you tell me you could raise my loan amount and run my credit?

Not to mention he was not available towards the end because he was moving into his new house and yeah I felt a little bitter about that too. It was like the world was conspiring against me.

And all I can think now is that this house just simply isn't meant to be.

And all I can do now is have faith in that. Have faith that God knows what he is doing and that he is working on a bigger better plan for me.

Because if I sit in the thought of losing the home prior to Florida, losing over $250,000, losing my construction home, I will probably go insane.

I have to admit what I am going through now is regretting selling my sweet little Dallas house in the first place. I shouldn't have sold it, I should have simply vacationed in Destin for a longer period of time.

The crazy thing actually is I had booked an AIRBNB in Destin for October of 2021. Because I thought, before I do something crazy like move there, let me spend a month and see if maybe a month of beach time a year is all I need. Because my family vacation time of one week wasn't enough for me.

But then I canceled this airbnb when I thought, NOPE I just know I want to live there.

Good job, way to go. Look at you now LOL.

Well we all make mistakes, I just made a very expensive one.

And I have no house to show for it.

I didn't just lose enough money to make someone's stomach hurt, I also lost the house I loved. I lost the place where my last memories of Loxi would ever remain.

I thought I was doing the right thing at the time, so I know that has to account for something. It's easy to be here now and look back and say "ok bad mistake" but at the time it wasn't one yet.

I had hope.

Of course if I knew then what I know now, I wouldn't have done it. I wouldn't have sold that charming house that Mikah, Loxi and I had built on love, I would have simply taken a longer vacation in Florida and saying this to be fair makes me feel ridiculous. But I was just so hell bent that Florida was right for me, so I deserve the way everything has panned out. But it all isn't bad, I'm not suggesting that I deserved bad, I just deserved the outcome and it has been both bad and good. Because I lost the construction house, I decided I have been simply too traumatized to buy a house right now. I'm going to rent and take time to figure all of this out.

It's not fun knowing I will have to move YET again, but I can't deal with buying and selling right now. The owner of this house I am going to rent is living out of the country and they might be coming back to live in their house after my one year lease is up, so be prepared for me to move soon.

sigh

But I'm excited to be home. Coming back here I know this was the right decision. I feel like myself again, I feel like I belong, I love my Texas people, and I love my Texas crazy weather and boy am I glad I'm not dealing with hurricanes because let me tell you...these Floridians are tough cookies for dealing with that. When I thought Charlie was going to hit the Panhandle and I saw my neighbors boarding up their windows and I missed my nephews' first birthday, I was a train wreck.

Did you know the Panhandle gets hurricanes AND tornadoes....YEAH not the deal I thought I was getting. I thought I was exchanging a tornado for a hurricane but you mean I gotta deal with BOTH?! Absolutely not.

And when Mikah and I had left just days later a tornado actually hit Destin. How crazy is that?

Do I miss the Florida house?

I do not.

I learned that no matter how much a house is worth it doesn't mean it turns into a home.

Home is where you make it and that is truly priceless.

I do hope the new owners love their home and have beautiful happy memories and to all of my Floridan's, I love y'all. Thank you for letting me live there and trying it out. Thank you for the beautiful beaches and how kind you all are.

I wish I could have been one of y'all. It was my dream for as long as I can remember. I think I was in my early twenties when I knew I wanted to live in Florida. It was a desire of mine for so long so I'm happy I at least tried it.

There was never a guarantee, nothing in life is.

I'm just grateful for all the lessons I learned.

PART VI

So what's next?

Leaving the AIRBNB, moving into my new rental I'm hoping I can make it a home for a year and maybe even hopefully two or more because if I don't have to move out of this new house girl trust me I won't. LOL.

I'm going to do the yard work. I'll mow, plant fall flowers, trim the bushes, take Loki for our walks, ride my bike again. Continue with my supplements, earth grounding, sun gazing, and doing breath work to help myself expel stress better.

I'm going to enjoy life as much as I can regardless of the hiccups.

I'm going to donate more, give back more, help the community more, and hopefully find the time to finish my romance novel that I hope to maybe be on your bookshelf one day.

I'm going to get my stuff out of the pods (finally), and prepare for fall decorating and share that journey with you all on my YouTube channel.

I'm going to be traveling to Canada very often to see my brother.

The other lesson I learned while I was gone was that I missed my brother. Yes I missed my sister in law and my niece and nephew but my brother is my person. I missed our Friday lunches and our funny face to face conversations and the inside jokes that only we understood. It was hard when I finally made my way back home to find out he's moving to Canada.

These life curveballs...

I mean, I don't even know what the hell is going on in my life but I gotta roll with the punches at this point. Just make sure to check in on me girl because who the hell knows what is going to happen next.

Thank you for saving me, for giving me a purpose when I needed it the most. When I lost Loxi you were my light. I will forever be grateful to you for this. For allowing me a space to just show my hauls and my decorating and having nice comments to read when I was spiraling. You made it all worth it.

Thank you for being kind to a stranger, to me. This book is dedicated to all of you. To all of my OG's who have been with me for more than eight years and watch me faithfully and comment and I don't always get to engage back with you.

I don't deserve you but I'm humbled I get to know you.

Thank you for loving Loxi.

She's our girl. I wish she knew she had love from all over the world and I can't help but wonder if she knows that now. Knows how many of you prayed for her when I asked you to.

Thank you for praying for me, for Mikah, for your grace when maybe I came across snappy or sad and down.

One thing I know for sure is that I always want to share bits of my life with you.

I don't ever want to change. I want to always share my hauls, and I want to decorate again and I want us to share ideas and knowing I have you makes me feel like at least that is the one thing that won't change about me.

I'm not a "move my cheese" kind of person. I don't like change, so I guess it shouldn't be a surprise I got to Florida and went into total shock. But you have always remained the same for me and that has been an important constant in my life that has kept me grounded.

Florida was a mess for me what can I say? I wish I had better news to report to you.

It's interesting when you are doing better and having good days in your life that you look back at yourself and the actions you took and sometimes feel embarrassed by them. Of course now I look back at how I reacted to that night, balling my eyes out at strangers in their own home looking happy while I'm sick and I think "ok you overreacted pretty badly there" I mean I wasn't dying.

I wasn't in the hospital receiving devastating news, I wasn't counting my last days; I could walk, talk, and overall while yes I was sick I still had generally decent health.

But I didn't feel that at that particular moment in my life. I felt so tired of it all and I simply snapped. So should I feel embarrassed to tell this story? Still a little yes if I am being honest. I lost my dog, I started to have panic attacks, my stomach issues got worse, I sold my beloved house with my beloved memories for a dream that turned into a nightmare for me. But was it even a nightmare? I had a roof over my head, running water, AC/Heat, food in the fridge and I'm telling a story about how I lost almost four hundred thousand dollars. Yes I am very grateful for the life the Lord blessed me with, but I'm also just simply telling the story of what I went through. How one thing after another just made me feel defeated.

It was an uphill battle that I lost very quickly.

Missing home, missing everything I had known for my entire life to start in a new place at 40 years old to face one issue after another in this new house. It wasn't something I could personally handle all on my own.

That's just me. I don't doubt for a second someone else in my shoes could have gracefully handled it way better than I ever could, no I don't doubt that at all.

I handle so much on my own that I only have so much in my tank to be able to handle the bad things so when they happen I am already feeling like I'm on a tightrope.

But that's what this story is all about. How I can look back now and know what I can do better next time. It's all I can do, it's all I have control over and I know life is going to do those funny things to me again and now I'm geared with a better understanding of myself, of what I can and candle handle and how to ask for help to alleviate some of the life pressures I simply can't do on my own.

How it's ok to ask for help and how it's ok to be human and to have bad days and that all I can truly do at the end of the day is my best on that day. And my best will simply vary and that's ok too.

But it's so easy to say that now, now that my mind isn't stressed, now that my body doesn't feel at its lowest, so very easy to say that.

Whelp…I tried. How many times have I said that now? Don't worry I'm just trying to convince myself not you.

Thank you for spending your hard earned money on this book that covers just two years of my life. I know it's not a novel but I felt I had to share this with you.

When I started this book and said I always envied the ones that say "I have been called to…" and they list out what they say God has called them to, this is why I wrote this book.

I just had this weird push to do this, so maybe that's God!

Maybe this small little book was my calling because despite what it appears sharing these moments is very hard for me to do. I don't like feeling vulnerable, knowing I'm opening myself up for possible attacks but if this book helps just one person then it was all worth it.

Know that you are not alone. This was the biggest one for me personally. I love life, I think there is so much beauty in it and I have always understood that bad things and unfortunate things will and can happen but knowing you're not alone...that is somehow the most comforting thing to experience.

You're not alone, and you don't have to let the bad things weigh you down. I let it weigh me down but I am also not going to be upset with myself either for how I reacted. It's done, it happened and there isn't anything I can do to change it. I can learn from it and I can decide how I deal with things from here on out.

I know we all go through stuff and my childhood was rough so I am very grateful for my life but losing Loxi just took a toll on me.

I never knew my soul could intertwine with another and it most definitely did with hers.

I think of the day I will get to see her again.

I think of standing there, hearing her running and waiting to see her run over the hill as I see her for the first time.

Does anyone else do this? Envision seeing their passed loved ones again?

It think about Loxi all the time. And Lolly. My two girls that I hope are all playing with your fur babies if you have one at the rainbow bridge.

But now I get to be here with Loki. How more lucky can I get? Loki is the snuggliest, cutest, hammiest, precious boy and I'm just speechless that I am the one that gets to have him and love him.

He's sitting here watching me as I type now with the funniest old man look on his face LOL.

My little Loki bear and you guys love him so much already. Such wonderful people in this world, and to know you exist is so very comforting.

I am so proud of myself for not settling with the panic or the pain. I'm glad I didn't roll over and just accept this as my fate. I'm proud that I fought for myself and worked to help and heal my body. I'm proud that I did what I thought was best for me even if maybe it was unconventional or risky. I'm proud of myself for going for my dream even though it didn't work. I'm proud of myself for accepting the defeat with the sell of my home to simply allow myself to move on and not be hard on myself and harbor all of this regret. I'm proud I didn't let it harden me.

I'm proud I fought back against the punches from life and I know I will continue to do it because life will continue to be life. It will have ups and downs and I know that's all about how I choose to experience those moments. How I choose to deal with stress.

I know I will make better choices in the future.

I finally know what it means to love myself. And that is another version of being healthy.

The last two years of my life was all about health and while I still have a lot to work on with my nutrients and making sure I'm consuming everything my body needs to thrive, this is the best my body has ever felt. So I'm clearly on the right path.

I'm excited for the small things to return to me once again. The mornings of turning on I Love Lucy, to brewing a pot of coffee I might either drink or just let it act as a candle and smell up the house. To let Loki out in the backyard while I head to my office and maybe write another chapter or two of my romance novel, to plan out all of my videos for you, and take my walks…that is what I live for. The smallest moments that mean so much to me.

I love watching people have massive social lives, and people who always seem to have a wedding to go to, or events and dinners and traveling. I love watching others live their life and this small one is mine. It might seem empty or boring to some, or beautiful to others because life is all about perspective. Just because I don't want to ride a Harley Davidson doesn't mean there isn't value in it. So just because all I want to do is be a homebody and decorate doesn't mean my life is empty. I do, however, want to push myself a little more. I don't want to always shop close to home, as silly as that sounds. I want to discover different places, and travel a little more now that my fear of flying is gone. But I will always want to come back home.

To Texas.

I have so much to be thankful for, grateful for, and I'm going to always try and make each day better than the last.

I have learned two things.

God is always with me and I am never alone.

I will always have problems, so I need to still enjoy life while I'm trying to solve them

To my YouTube Subscribers,

Thank you for being kind to me. Leaving me all the sweetest kindest comments that made more of an impact than you know even if you didn't get a response, I saw it. For looking forward to my videos. For praying for me and my family. For loving me. For loving Mikah, Loxi and Loki.

You gave me a purpose when I desperately needed one. How could I possibly ever repay you?

I made it through these past two years because of you.

It's such a wonderful world where I can share something I love with someone who loves it too and we have that common bond. It feels nice to just have a passion to share that you know someone else feels the same way about. You're my boos, and I love you.

I can't imagine what I must like through your eyes but through mine you're my safe haven.

I know a lot of you see the bad comments and you always come to my defense and I don't want that to be your experience. I want you to always come to my channel and it be a time for you where you feel good and safe. I know there will always be someone watching and judging not just me but anyone who chooses to put their lives out on social media. It comes with the territory so for you to watch and be kind to me means everything to me.

I am so thankful to know people like you exist in this world.

Thank you.

And to you Loxi Blue,

Losing you was the hardest thing I ever had to go through, yet I am so grateful because it is what finally put me on a path to heal myself properly.

I love you. I know you came here to heal me from Lolly's loss, to love me and to help me and I wish I could squish your faces with kisses but I rest knowing you are exactly where you need to be. I picture you with a sparkle in your beautiful blue eyes, your blue coat perfect, fluffy and shiny, the white of your chest as immaculate as snow. I picture you running, panting and smiling with pure joy. I picture you sometimes coming down to earth and crawling into bed with me without me even knowing to watch over me. I picture you with so many friends, and so many treats with days full of sunshine and adventures. I picture you wearing your plaid scarf I made you during the winter. I picture you with the most beautiful crown on your head. And I'm lucky I get to picture you at all. I'm lucky I got to know of your existence.

But for now we are all sending you our love because you captured our hearts.

Be a good girl up there, no back and forth shenanigans we know you are capable of. I'm sure Lolly showed you the ropes and you're probably a rainbow bridge professional by now. I can't wait until we see each other again.

Thank you for all your unconditional love you gave to me. Thank you for being with me during the rough times, the best times, the cold times when the power went out during Covid and we ran out of wood to burn. Thank you for how incredibly loving and gentle you were. For all the times you watched me cry in bed and you laid quietly next to me because you wanted to comfort me the only way you knew how. Thank you for bringing so much light into my life. So much of my life has changed because of you. You will never be just a dog. You are so much more to me.

I healed because of you. I became better because of you. My life changed because of you. I hope I loved you the way you deserved. I hope you had fun with me and Mikah. I hope you're waiting for me because I'm waiting for you.

I love you, my darling Loxi girl.